D0084587

Light, Bright, and Damned Near White

Recent titles in
Race and Ethnicity in Psychology

Sources of Stress and Relief for African American Women
Catherine Fisher Collins

Playing with Anger: Teaching Coping Skills to African American Boys through Athletics and Culture
Howard C. Stevenson Jr., editor

The Psychology of Prejudice and Discrimination, Volumes I-IV
Jean Lau Chin, editor

Light, Bright, and Damned Near White

Biracial and Triracial Culture in America

STEPHANIE ROSE BIRD

Race and Ethnicity in Psychology
Jean Lau Chin, Series Editor

Westport, Connecticut
London

Library of Congress Cataloging-in-Publication Data

Bird, Stephanie Rose, 1960–
Light, bright, and damned near white : biracial and triracial culture in America / Stephanie Rose Bird.
p. cm. — (Race and ethnicity in psychology, ISSN 1543–2203)
Includes index.
ISBN 978–0–275–98954–5 (alk. paper)
1. Ethnicity. 2. Ethnopsychology. 3. Blacks—Race identity. 4. Whites—Race identity. 5. Race awareness. 6. Race relations. I. Title.
GN495.6.B56 2009
305.8—dc22 2008039563

British Library Cataloguing in Publication Data is available.

Library of Congress Catalog Card Number: 2008039563
ISBN: 978–0–275–98954–5
ISSN: 1543–2203

First published in 2009

Praeger Publishers, 88 Post Road West, Westport, CT 06881
An imprint of Greenwood Publishing Group, Inc.

www.praeger.com

Printed in the United States of America

The paper used in this book complies with the Permanent Paper Standard issued by the National Information Standards Organization (Z39.48–1984).

10 9 8 7 6 5 4 3 2 1

With hope for a more enlightened future.
Dedicated with love to my husband Damian
and our children: Colin, Liam, Olivia, and Ian.

And, with heartfelt thanks for sharing the wisdom of
our collective past:
to my ancestors.

Contents

Series Foreword *ix*

Preface *xi*

1 Premixed—Premeasured: Populace of the New World 1

2 Too Light to Be Black, Too Dark to Be White: Who Is Passing for What? 11

3 Tan Territory: Separating Fact, Fiction, and Fantasy 27

4 Some of America's Best-Known Triracial Groups 43

5 Bricolage: Constructed Identities of *Les Gens de Couleur Libre* and Cane River Negroes 59

6 From Italian Explorers to Sicilian Contandini and Biracial Royals: The Mixed-Race Experience as Illustrated by the Italian Diaspora 77

7 Black, White, and Red All Over American History: Coming Together yet Remaining Apart 87

8 The Stolen Generations: When Things Really Go Wrong 101

9 Profiles of Triumph and Courage 109

10 The State of the Mixed Union: What's Happening in the Government, on Campus, on the Internet, and in the News 123

11 A Tool Box for Change: News to Use 135

Index *147*

Series Foreword

When we look at diversity, we tend to view it in terms of neat categories of individuals by race and ethnicity. We talk of whites, blacks, Asian, and Latinos as distinct groups and categories. *Light, Bright, and Damned Near White* throws these concepts to the wind. It challenges us to acknowledge how society and nations have been oppressive to triracial and biracial individuals through its absence of categories for mixed race people. In doing so, it has stolen their very identities by forcing them to choose between components of their racial and ethnic origins.

What are you? This is the ultimate question we ask of people to find out their racial and ethnic origins, expecting them to pick one of the categories we have defined in our minds. The privilege for whites is this is not a question they need to answer. For racial and ethnic minority group individuals, this becomes the question to enable the questioner to define one's identity; it is emotionally charged because the question is often used to question the legitimacy of belonging and the validity of identity. For biracial and triracial individuals, this experience is even more intense because they do not fit in the neat categories of the questioner; they are ambiguous in their appearance.

The book is rich with personal vignettes of those from many combinations of race and ethnicity; the vast possible combinations demonstrate just how complex this experience is. In portraying the anguish this question stirs up, the author communicates the issues of identity, ostracism, rejection, shame and the denial it evokes—individuals who do not belong to either group, are not accepted by either group. The books asserts the importance of turning this around—by establishing new categories of identities for mixed race people that defy those arbitrarily thrust upon them. It is the basis for establishing pride and strength, validity and acceptance of themselves.

The book traces the historical evolution of triracial and biracial people dating back as far back as 1607 "when three ships sailed into the Chesapeake Bay, stopping at Jamestown, Virginia, to establish the first English colony in the New World"—Native women were enslaved, raped, or seduced by white men (p. 4). Yet, their offspring were not recognized as biracial. There are countless examples of how laws and government sanctioned active attempts to separate, denounce, criminalize, and punish those who dared to intermarry or intermix. As nations, we have not recognized the existence of triracial and biracial individuals in our midst when we refuse to allow multiple categories in our census count, or when we legislate anti-miscegenation laws and arbitrarily decide who is white vs. who is not. This history shows that triracial and biracial people have been invisible amidst their heightened visibility that played havoc with their psyche.

In eloquent prose, Bird writes about and questions the "purity of race," "one-drop rule," "passing as white," and other such concepts that box people in, produce anguish, and pose adverse consequences for mixed race people. These concepts are inherently oppressive to mixed race people because being white is valued and dominant, and entitles individuals to the fruits of society. In tracing the centuries of our failure to accept the notion of racial mixtures, Bird suggests that it is time for change. Societies, governments, and nations must apologize for the trauma inflicted upon mixed race people. Mixed race people must heal from all the wounds inflicted upon their identity by a society unwilling to accept the reality of racial mix. She calls refers to "stolen generations" in Australia, where settlers tore Aborigine children from their families because they were not of the right color—white or black. In speaking to strength and validation, Bird insists that triracial and biracial people don't need to choose. Instead, she offers and creates many new categories of identity to reflect the complexity of their origins—Cablinasian used by Tiger Woods to capture his multiple origins. Bird urges triracial and biracial people to move from being objects of curiosity, stigma, discrimination, and rejection, to symbols of triumph and courage, belonging and acceptance, pride and strength.

Jean Lau Chin

Preface

What are you?

Could there be a more loaded question? I can think of hundreds of answers personally: a woman, an artist, a writer, a Chicagoan, a mother, a nature lover, kind of quiet, funny at times . . . but, this would not answer "the" question, as it is intended. I have only been confused as a "White lady" once by some Côte d'Ivoirian braiders that I think were just having a good laugh at my expense, in French no less, as they discussed my "ugly" hairstyle.

Clearly, I am a person of color. Some just want to know what exact blend I am on the painter's palette—in other words, which colors have been added together to create the skin of me? Are you Puerto Rican, part Aboriginal, part Middle Eastern, Jamaican, Caribbean, Fijian, or perhaps mixed with north or south East Indian—these are more common to what my particular looks generate. They are actually the sorts of answers people give to their own questions about my identity.

> I don't know where I come from. When people ask me, I have to stop and wonder, what it is they really want to know about me. Do they want to know where I was born, where I grew up, where I have lived as an adult, where I live now? It troubles me to be scattered, so fragmented so far removed from a center. I am all and I am nothing. At the same time.
>
> —Meri Nana-Ama Danquah (Ghanaian, African-born American)[1]

HAIR AND IDENTITY

In reaction to these inquiries, some of us do things to alter ourselves, some of this is done to fit in, while others create selective identities, which will be discussed later. I use to lie in the sun to become darker, so I wasn't asked too many questions. Yellow is a pretty, sunny color but doesn't feel good used as a pejorative when it is somehow suggesting you are "other" or, worse still, when a bully nastily proclaims, "You are the color of piss."

Hair is a very politically loaded accessory to a woman's form especially. My hair, which often is mistaken for weave no matter how I wear it, is another source of confusion to the Identity Inspectors. My hair made me seem "other"—it grew too long, too fast and didn't revert (to a nappy state), so to speak, when it was wet. Instead, it resembled a Jerri Curl perm (California Curl ™) . . . "She got baby doll hair," I remember hearing one day when I was running home through the rain. I'd also hear through the wind . . . "she got White people hair." People stared at the end product when I was at predominately African American beauty salons. None of it felt good, though it could have been taken as some sort of weird compliment.

Now, I wear my hair in long dreadlocks that almost touch my butt. Still, people think those are fake as well, asking me how often I have to get them done. I have learned to accept that I will receive questions no matter how much I tan or change my hairstyle, so I refrain from both activities. Instead, I have begun to pursue for myself my identity, utilizing DNA testing and in-depth genealogy in the process. Moreover, I have undertaken a spiritual journey—this, perhaps the most meaningful step of all.

Most of us on the receiving end of *the* question prefer to be left alone. "What am I?" I am what I be—a human, a woman, a mom, a writer, a little too heavy right now, a water lover, and a bit peeved that you feel compelled to question my identity.

RAINBOW PEOPLE

For so long there has been quiet on the racial scene. Finally, we weren't particulate, at least not mulatto, octoroon, quadroon, griffe, or zambo—we were just Black, end of story. But truthfully, mixed people of all types and histories have always had similar characteristics thrust upon them. The most common designation imposed on multiracial people of all ancestries is the idea that they are fragmented human beings. Words such as *mulatto* and *octoroon* have referred to those origins in Africa, while for indigenous Americans, *mixed blood* and *half-breed* are more common. Latinos from the United States utilize *mestizo,* as do some Indian/White admixtures.

Regardless of the reference, none of these are terms of endearment to us. All of them perpetuate the quack-science notion of blood divisions being a real way to quantify and fractionate a human being. In a race-obsessed world, these fractions support the notion that the multiracial individual is somehow less than a whole person;[2] thus they too are terms that should be avoided.

Idiotic pseudoscience was supposed to establish a theoretic framework that ordered, categorized, and explained the variety that exists in humans as well as to distinguish superior races from the inferior. In this type of hierarchy, Indians were in competition with Black people of African descent, as the "lowest race of mankind" in what was called "the great chain of being" by early Eurocentric social scientists.[3]

Half and Half or Black and Proud?

Remember the anthem James Brown popularized, "Say it loud; I'm Black, and I'm proud"? Well, if I had to do this thing called life again, given a choice, I'd chose to be Black, again and again. Because I know, as a painter, black is the sum total of all colors. Unfortunately, most people believe black is created from itself—out of its own tube—black is black—thus if you are Black, you are monoracial. Nothing could be further from the truth.

In the anthology on race, *Half and Half*, Danzy Senna, author of *Caucasia: A Novel*, goes further to express her displeasure with the designation "multicultural" to describe disparate groups of people:

> In South Africa, during apartheid, they had 14 different types of colored. But we decided on this one word, "multiracial," to describe, in effect a whole nation of diverse people who have absolutely no relation, cultural or otherwise to one another.[4]

Another writer, Meri Nana-Ama Danquah, describes his painful recognition coming from Africa to an African American community where he learned that the many shades of blackness are hard to hold in a singular term for a group of diverse people such as Americans who identify as Black:

> Being black male made the transition from Africa to America extremely difficult because it introduced another complex series of boundaries. In a racially divided country, it isn't enough for an immigrant to know how to float in the mainstream. You have to know how to retreat to your margin, where to place your hyphen. You have to know that you are no longer just yourself, you are now an Asian American, a Latin American, an Irish American, or, in my case, a black American. (Only recently has the label changed to African American.) At the time of my emigration in the early 1970s, Washington, D.C., a predominately black city, was awash in a wave of Afrocentricity. Dashikis draped brown shoulders and the black-fisted handle of an Afro-pick proudly stuck out in many a back pant's pocket. However, despite all the romanticizing and rhetoric about unity and brotherhood, there was a curtain of sheer hostility hanging between black Americans and black Africans.[5]

THE GREAT MIX-MATCH

Basically, because of conditions that began with the earliest settlers, White genes continuously disseminated through the Black community via the marriage of mulattoes to Africans. Only a few Blacks, like the Gullah/GeeChee people of the seacoast islands of Georgia and South Carolina, escaped the dilution of the African genes. More than two centuries of racial mixing between masters, slaves, and lovers, both White and Indian, had produced a population of Black people more racially mixed than pure. An African from Ghana coming into this type of history might not be aware what had gone on behind the scenes. Moreover, many Africans felt they had more of a right to the title of African American. The two disparate cultures did not mesh together as easily as an outsider to the Black communities on both sides of the Atlantic would have thought.

So, we have Black history; his-story; her-story; Anglo, Latino, Asian, and Native American history, but what of the history of the rainbow people?

Have they always been around, or are they a new phenomenon? When did race mixing begin? What is it properly called? Are there distinctive groups of multiracial, biracial, or triracial people outside the United States, too? Where do they live in the United States? What do they look like? What do they do? How did they come to exist?

If you have wondered about these things, *Light, Bright, and Damned Near White* is the book for your curious mind. Part memoir, part sociological and anthropological musing, as well as historical overview, this book has some ground to cover. *Light, Bright, and Damned Near White* examines triracial, biracial, and multiethnic identity from various times in history and varied perspectives, particularly the one I know best—a very personal one.

NOTES

1. Meri Nana-Ama Danquah, "Life as an Alien," in *Half and Half: Writers on Growing Up Biracial and Bicultural* (anthology), ed. Claudine Chiawei O'Hearn (New York: Pantheon Books, 1998), 99.
2. Laurie Mengel, "Triples—The Social Evolution of a Multiracial Pan-ethnicity: An Asian American Perspective," in *Rethinking Mixed Race,* ed. D. Parker and M. Song (London: Pluto Press, 2001), 101.
3. M. Annette Jaimes, "Some Kind of Indian: On Race Eugenics and Mixed Blood" in *American Mixed Race,* ed. N. Zack (London: Rowman and Littlefield, 1995), 134.
4. Danzy Senna, "Mulatto Millennium," in *Half and Half: Writers on Growing Up Biracial and Bicultural* (anthology), ed. Claudine Chiawei O'Hearn (New York: Pantheon Books, 1998), 22–23.
5. Danquah, "Life as an Alien," 99.

CHAPTER 1

Premixed—Premeasured: Populace of the New World

EARLY U.S. CENSUS DEFINITIONS OF *MULATTO*

The mulatto as the term is used in this study, includes all those members of the Negro race with a visible admixture of white blood. Thus used, the word is a general term to include all Negroes of mixed ancestry regardless of the degree of intermixture.

—*U.S. Census Report, 1910, Population Vol. 1, p. 189*

BRINGING TOGETHER THE POLES

At an early age, I recall being frustrated with the simplistic categories ascribed to race. My interest in biological anthropology came swiftly of unknown origin, perhaps it was as simple as having numerous *National Geographic* magazines and a few encyclopedias on hand at home to browse whenever desired. I remember looking for myself in the four distinct anthropological categories: Caucasoid, Negroid, Mongoloid, and Australoid. I looked at the illustrations and read over how we were described, if we were considered members of any given group. Clearly, more than anywhere else I belonged in the Negroid group, but looking at my family, knowing my family history, and to some extent looking in the mirror, I knew these anthropological categories were doing a shallow job of telling a complete story.

In a country, whose cultural orientation is built around the sharp divisions marked by polar the opposite colors, Black and White, people whose ethnicity combines these two groups have struggled to assert their collective identity. In the media for example, Black and White people are pitted against one another, portrayed as being in opposition visually and culturally.

CENSUS 2000

After a great deal of activism by groups such as the MAVIN Foundation and the Association of Multiethnic Americans (AMEA), which will be discussed at length later in the book, the U.S. Census added a new category to ethnic identification in the year 2000. Now we can click the multiracial box, but for many desiring greater specificity to honor complex heritage, one box is not enough.

COMPLICATIONS OF COMPLEXIONS

To envision the genesis of the color complex we all suffer with, its best to return to the year 1607, when three ships sailed into the Chesapeake Bay, stopping at Jamestown, Virginia, to establish the first English colony in the New World.

Native Americans watched the pale-faced strangers clear and cut their forests, build fortresses, and plant crops. More White men followed, but to survive, the tiny settlement also needed women and a reliable supply of cheap labor. Yet over a decade passed before the first White women disembarked at Jamestown. Closer to the arrival of the men, in the same year in fact that the first White men arrived at Jamestown, the first shipment of Africans arrived as well.

In a New World and different era, what might have been unimaginable in Europe and Africa was an everyday occurrence in the wilds of what was to become our country. Race-mixing became widespread as Europeans, Africans, and Native Americans came together producing a kaleidoscopic array of skin tones, types, and features. Still, the primary race groupings were categorized and differed sharply in their civil liberties and political freedoms. Subtle variations in appearance held enormous consequences in many cases, especially among Negroes.[1]

HOUSTON, WE HAVE A PROBLEM

Predictably, the issue of interculturalism, triracial and biracial culture, arose the second seafaring people arrived in the United States.

It was the mass meeting of the cultured and primitive peoples, brought about as a result of the period of discoveries, that gave rise to the mixed-blood races with a status different in some respects from that of either of the parent races; and so gave rise, in some cases at least, to a special social and racial set of problems.[2]

Here, a ripe situation presented itself for meetings, taking, mating with, marrying, kidnapping, or raping women of different ethnicities.

After the lengthy transatlantic voyage to an unimaginable destination, the English sailors arrived in the New World desperate for rest and relaxation. Native women were seduced or raped, and before long, the first generation of blue-eyed, light-skinned Indians appeared among the local tribes.[3]

The Native American woman was a likely, though well-guarded, subject and somewhat empowered by knowing her geography and how to utilize elaborate intertribal networks and affiliations. Women of African descent, some already mixed during the enslavement "seasoning" process, in places like Santo Domingo, Dominican Republic, Jamaica, Trinidad, and elsewhere in the Caribbean, some multilingual, bicultural (Arabic, English, and various African-language speakers) and mestizo, were accustomed to European and other types of men. Dutch traders brought Africans to Virginia from Santo Domingo in the West Indies, where Negroes had been enslaved on sugar plantations since the 1500s. Among this group of Africans were a few who were English speaking and some who had been converted to Christianity.

The early White Virginians, unfamiliar with the nuances of slavery, released religious converts following a specified term of service. So, from the earliest days of the colonies, there were free Negroes and free people of color living here.[4] These and other people in similar social circumstances became entangled with the White man's desire to procure women for sexual and other needs as well as becoming ensnared in an inflated sense of male privilege.

WHERE'S THE PURITY?

The anthropological categories of humans assumes a very flawed theory—that purity exists. When there is purity, along the lines of an entirely unique species, then we can begin our categorizations. People would feel at ease, clicking a box and identifying with their allotted group if purity was real. However, since the earliest of times, there have been ongoing circumstances that have brought diverse people together under one colorful roof. This may be the result of trading—something human beings love to do. Stepping out of one's bounds and marrying someone not from their group of origin. Falling in lust and creating children that are a mixture of two or more cultures is another way, as is traveling between clans and tribes for annual gatherings and celebrations. Of course, then, too, there are the seafarer's who really mixed things up. In short, precious few humans have lived in pure isolation from all others long enough to form a distinctive race.

It would be 12 years, for example, before the Virginia Company settlers of Jamestown would receive the addition of White women to their all-male communities. Purportedly, many of the imported women were indentured servants or of ill-repute, degenerate, prostitutes, escapees from mental institutions, and criminals, though some were also very fine women.[5] Most of the others suitable for the group were already well-established and situated in English society.

On the other hand, as I've stated, many of the enslaved women were already encultured before arriving in America; some were mestizo or Métis and thus seemed to have some cultural relationship to the men. The Creole woman in particular was often seen as sophisticated, attractive, and graceful, particularly the highly admixed type that use to be called octoroon or quadroon. These women seem to have stirred a bestial attraction in White men, and from early on, one way or another, there were progeny from such unions.

THE QUESTION OF BIRACIALISM

The assumption of biracial culture is that there are two distinct races. The more promising triracial or multiracial designation suggests there is a profusion of cultures that have come together out of these main anthropological groups. The neat categories begin to disintegrate, however, when we are reminded that from their earliest days on North American shores, explorers and colonizers became sexually involved with Native American women and the enslaved, as well as free, people of various colors and cultures, brought here to work.

WHAT COLOR LINE?

In social affairs, the color line between the Whites and the mixed-blood race is neither hard nor fast.[6] Many of the so-called Whites are tinged with Negro or Indian blood.[7]

The colonizers themselves were not of the lily white brand. They came from Portugal and Spain as well as Italy and had mixed with Northern Europeans or with Middle Eastern strains, particularly from places like Morocco and Turkey. The descendants of these people are particularly noted in the Melungeon communities of Appalachia and the Ozarks, the southeast and east coast of the United States.

Previously, I demonstrated how the early mixing of the Virginia Company settlers with Native American women makes it virtually impossible to find an east or southeast coast Native American group that is absolutely "pure" racially rather than being an amalgamation of Indo-European and sub-Saharan African.

PREMIXED POPULATIONS: HEADED FOR SHORES COLORED BLACK AND WHITE

In many of the Negroes brought as slaves to America, there was already the penetration of Caucasian ancestry. The great majority of enslaved individuals, well above 50 percent, came from the West Coast of Africa. A few came from central Congo. A few, like my own people, were from southern Africa, and fewer still were actual Bushmen. Possibly 50 percent were already mixed, and 1 percent spoke Arabic before arrival on New World shores.[8]

With the lengthy history of invasions, wars, trading, and migrations of both Indo-Europeans and sub-Saharan Africans, it is also practically impossible to find a substantial number of ethnically pure Whites or Blacks. So before we even started the proliferation of miscegenation, writing, laws, and theories of the Victorian era, we were already discussing people who were mixed by varying degrees and throughout the genetic spectrum of Asian/Native American, Indo-European, sub-Saharan African, and Pacific Islanders' input of the great seafaring people. Only, we didn't have a tool as definitive as DNA ancestry tests, which will be discussed at length later to flesh out or illustrate the story.

While the group generally referred to as biracial is a complex territory to explore , there are also long-standing groups, referred to historically as Tri-Racial and—in older literature— as Tri-Racial Isolates, whose heritage affords the opportunity to explore what a triracial or multiracial culture might be. Triracial groups have blended White and Black with the addition of various Native American nations.

This book explores the historic and contemporary issues involved with triracial, biracial, and multiracial American heritage. I will also examine such occurrences abroad, pointing to the "Stolen Generation" of Australia, the case of the "coloreds" in apartheid South Africa, and the miscegenation within the noble families of Europe.

Finally, *Light, Bright, and Damned Near White* attempts to assist readers in their search for ancestry. Woven throughout are the psychological and sociological issues raised by the assertion of multiracial identity, as opposed to homogenous cultural identification as Black, White, or Indian.

In many ways, this book mirrors my journey of understanding the heritage and ancestry of my people. I have focused the conversation primarily around the triracial triangle of people identified as Black, White, and Native American, though we focus on Australian Aborigines, European, Latino/Latina/Hispanic, and African cultures in specific conversations throughout.

My primary interests here are folklore, storytelling, anthropology, and sociology rather than other scientific or philosophic inquiry. My goal is to educate, converse, and bring further understanding to the history and contemporary happenings in mixed-race culture. For that reason, I am not challenging the issue of race, per se, or mixed-raced groups, leaving that to others, as it is a lively debate. My way is seeing this book as a capsule full of varied ethnicities with a story to tell. I do not support the full theory of monoracialism because our duration of life as humans on this earth, with all of its opportunity to mix with one another, makes it inherently flawed. I do believe in ethnic identification as a form of culture and cultural belonging.

Chart 1. Early Mixed-Race Classifications:

French Classification of Colored People circa 1854[9]

Sacatra	griffe and negress
Griffe	Negro and mulatto
Marabon	mulatto and griffe
Mulatto	white and Negro
Quadroon	white and mulatto
Metif	white and Quadroon
Meamelouc	white and metif
Quarteron	white and meamelouc
Sang-mele	white and quarteron

Chart 2. Early Mixed-Race Classifications:[10]

Mulatto	Negro and white
Quadroon	mulatto and white
Octoroon	quadroon and white
Cascos	mulatto and mulatto
Sambo	mulatto and Negro
Mango	sambo and Negro
Mustifee	octoroon and white
Mustifino	mustifee and white[11]

USAGE OF THE TERMS *BIRACIAL* AND *MULTIRACIAL*

> Two human groups never meet but they mingle their blood.
>
> —Melville J. Herskovits

As groups, races are not stable entities, yet when Americans hear the word *race,* they generally think in terms of the Black and White dichotomy. The Black and White racial dichotomy imposes a myopic linguistic convention, which holds that everyone belongs to a race but that there are only two kinds of races, Negro and Caucasian. Today, as more people venture to take DNA ancestry tests, they are finding that the meaning of

Black, White, red, yellow, or brown American in terms of ethnicity and heritage is deep and far more complex than a color to signify race could ever adequately describe.

The danger of assigning too much weight to any given race as a signifier of anything of import is that great prejudice from dominant racial groups in any given time, territory, or situation occurs because false doctrines and assumptions about racial superiority and inferiority quickly arise. This grows prejudice—something that we as a nation continue to struggle with.

While we look toward the past to identify the players and cultures that have helped establish this conversation, this is very much a forward-looking book whose message is more concerned with inclusively than exclusivity. *Light, Bright, and Damned Near White* will hopefully lead to greater understanding of ourselves as a multiracial, multiethnic, and multicultural group of inner-related people. We will consider the notion of inner-relatedness, what that means, who we are, and how we can set about healing and moving forward while keeping the desired aspects of our multicultural identity intact.

In this book, I am aligned with the definition of the terms *biracial* and *multiracial* set forth by Naomi Zack, herself triracial, in her anthology *Race and Mixed Race* (Philadelphia, PA: Temple University Press, 1995). The terms are sometimes used interchangeably. Many people who are biracial have a parent who is also mixed, which brings about the triracial individual.

Biracial—Refers to someone with two socially and phenotypically distinct racial ancestries, one coming from each parent. It can also refer to multigenerational history of prior miscegenation. The looser definition moves one away from the notion of being particulate humans and works towards a holistic vision.

Hispanic—All Hispanics are basically triracial; their ancestral populations being European, African, and Native American (north or south). However, the proportion of genes Hispanics received from ancestral populations varies greatly.[12] Hispanics are a broad and growing community currently representing 17 percent of the United States Population. The ethnic category "Hispanic" was defined by the Office of Management and Budget in 1978 as people or descendants of people from Latin American countries or other Spanish-speaking cultures.[13] This definition includes thousands and perhaps millions more Americans with European-Spanish ancestry that have not identified as Hispanic, including myself.

Latino—A clarification on the Hispanic designation that is designed to be more inclusive. The term *Latino* encompasses European Spaniards but is also inclusive of all those from Latin American countries who speak Spanish and those who do not.[14]

Mestizo—This group soon became a numerically important element in the population. Later, there were large numbers of enslaved black Africans introduced from the West Coast. Unions between the Portuguese and Black women began with the first introduction of African-descended peoples. These diverse African groups mixed with Indians and were called Zambos.[15]

Métis—It was a triangular mixture of unknown proportions of Portuguese, Indian, and Negro admixtures that produced what are called Métis.[16] In Brazil, the Métis form a middle class residing between the White aristocracy and the Negro and Indian populations, much like the pre-Louisiana Purchase les *gens de couleur libre* (discussed at length in chapter 5).[17]

Multiracial—Includes the biracial person and others blending two or more diverse ancestries, for example, African, Native American, and European, such as Latino and Hispanics, also called mestizo. It is also a term that acknowledges that the suppression of multiracial heritage in this country limits knowledge about an individuals racial origins. The topic of racially mixed people provides us with a vehicle for exploring ideologies surrounding race, race relations and the role of social sciences in the deconstruction of race. On the whole I am referring to multiracial individuals in this book as "mixed race."

It is confusing to our linear models of identity to consider that a multiracial or triracial (African, Caucasian, and Native American) who looks African American self-identifies as multiracial, whereas a similar person self-identifies as a monoracial African American, yet these and other conundrums will arise while envisioning the diverse array of racial and ethnic types explored in these pages.

NOTES

1. Kathy Russell, Midge Wilson, and Ronald Hall, *The Color Complex: The Politics of Skin Color Among African Americans* (New York: Anchor Books/Random House, 1993), 9.

2. Edward Byron Reuter, "The Mulatto in the United States: Including a Study of the Role of Mixed-Blood Races Throughout the World" (Ph.D. diss., University of Chicago, 1918), 27.

3. Russell, Wilson, and Hall, *The Color Complex,* 10.

4. Ibid.

5. Reuter, "The Mulatto in the United States," 127.

6. *The Chicago Defender,* January 15, 1916.

7. James Bryce, *South America: Observations and Impressions* (Macmillian, 1920), 479–480.

8. Ibid., 130.

9. Frederick Law Olmsted, *A Journey in the Seaboard Slave States With Remarks on Their Economy* (New York: Dix and Edwards, 1856), 583.

10. C. B. Davenport, *Heredity of Skin Color in Negro-White Crosses* (Washington, D.C.: Carnegie Institution of Washington, 1918), 27.

11. Reuter, "The Mulatto in the United States."

12. Bernardo Bertoni, Bruce Budowle, Monica Sans, Sara A, Barton, and Ranajit Chakraborty, "Admixture in Hispanics: Distribution of Ancestral Population Contributions in the Continental United States," *Human Biology* 75 (2003): 1–11.

13. Jayne O. Ifekwunigwe, ed., *Mixed Race Studies: A Reader* (London: Routledge, 2004), 16.
14. Ibid.
15. Reuter, "The Mulatto in the United States," 28.
16. Ibid., 33.
17. Ibid., 35.

CHAPTER 2

Too Light to Be Black, Too Dark to Be White: Who Is Passing for What?

Many people become exclusive, isolating the other parts of their known ethnic identity to gain membership to a seemingly monoracial group. For some this is a political act.

A MULATTO MILLENNIUM?

In the anthology *Half and Half: Writers on Growing Up Biracial and Bicultural,* edited by Claudine Chiavivei O'Hearn, a variety of writers share personal reflections on nearly every conceivable type of ethnic or cultural mix. Not entirely chuffed, in "The Mulatto Millennium," Danzy Senna laments what she calls "mulatto fever":

"But, with all due respect to the multicultural movement, I cannot tell a lie. I was a black girl. Not your ordinary black girl, if such a thing exists, but rather, born to a black-Mexican father, and a face that harkens to Andalusia, not Africa. I was born in 1970, when 'Black' described a people bonded not by shared complexion or hair texture but by a shared history." She points to the one-drop rule, that suggested any portion of African heritage made one "Black" and retorts, "You told us all along that we had to call ourselves Black because of this so-called 'one drop.' Now, that we don't have to anymore, we choose to. Because Black is beautiful. Because Black is not a burden, but a privilege.[1]

Senna, who is technically biracial and bicultural expresses disdain for those who identify as mulatto. She cites the book by populist Jim Hightower, *There's Nothing in the Middle of the Road but Yellow Stripes and Dead Armadillos,* as a metaphor for the mulatto centrist mentality.

As seen at the beginning of this chapter, in the old days, we were much more divided, at least in names ascribed, than today—*mulatto* was only the beginning in terms of the 14 other words used to describe the different types of mixed-race individuals we saw in the first chapter. Utilizing some of the old-fashioned ways of viewing each type of mixed-race person as belonging to a specific group with unique attributes (though simply describing mixed-raced people in an elaborate way), Senna utilizes the antiquated naming style, categorizing each type of mixed person as a separate species, with tongue-in-cheek humor and social critique at the same time:

1. *Standard mulatto*—white mother, black father . . . often raised in isolation from its kind. Does not discover his or her black identity until college at which time there is a drastic change in dress and speech patterns.
2. *African American*—the most common form of mulatto in North America. Not often described as mixed but is nevertheless, triracial, being African, European, and Native American. May come in any skin tone.
3. *Jewlatto*—second most prevalent form on North American Continent. This breed is made from co-mingling of Jews and Blacks. Common to have a white father and black mother, raised in a diverse setting such as Berkeley or Greenwich Village, or the town where I live, Oak Park. Famous Jewlattos include Lenny Kravitz, Lisa Bonet, and their love child Zoe.
4. *Mestizo*—triracial, black, white, plus the addition of Latino or Native American. Confused children mistaken for Italian, Arab, Mexican, Jewish, East Indian, Native American, or Puerto Rican. Passes as a third "pure" distinct race such as Latino or Hispanic.
5. *Gelatto*—Italian American and African American mixture. Usually lives in strictly Italian neighborhood if white father like Bensonhurst or black neighborhood if father is black like Flatbush (both in New York).
6. *Cultural Mulatto or Fauxlatto*—Americans born after 1967 who assume race that it is not necessarily a part of their genetic heritage such as a "wigger." Fauxlatto is impersonating a mulatto so slightly differs from a cultural mulatto. She uses singer Jamiroqui for an example.
7. *Blulatto*—a highly rare breed of blue blood mulattos who can trace their lineage back to the Mayflower or belong to the Daughters of the American Revolution. Mother is almost always white, father black, highly educated parents divorced or separated . . . may be angry . . . proceed with caution.
8. *Negratto*—raised to identify as black but can be any mixture. Suppresses cultural aspects that seem white. Usually more militant that their darker counterparts talks in slang, has great disgust for mulatto movement.
9. *Cablinasian*—rare exotic found mostly in California. Mother of mixtures—Asian, American Indian, Black, and Caucasian. Show mulatto with great performance skills; does not answer to the name Black.

10. *Tomatto*—a mixed person who behaves like an Uncle Tom. May hold positions of power; touted as symbol of diversity in otherwise all white settings. Light-skinned, mixed features, even with two black parents.[2]

WHAT COLORS ARE BLACK IN AMERICA?

In a taped interview conducted by a blind, Black anthropologist, a Black man nearly 90 years old said:

> Now, you must understand that this is just a name we have. I am not black and you are not black either, if you go by the evidence of your eyes . . . anyway, black people are all colors. White people don't look all the same way, but there's more different kinds of us than there is of them. Then too, there is a certain state (at) which you cannot tell who is white and who is black. Many of the people I see who are thought of as black could just as well be white in their appearance. Many of the white people I see are black as far as I can tell by the way they look. Now, that's it for looks. Looks don't mean much. The things that make us different is how we think. What we believe is important, the ways we look at life.[3]

ONE-DROP RULE

To be Black in the United States not even half of one's ancestry must be African Black. The nation's answer to the question, Who is Black? has long been that a Black person is any person with any known African Black ancestry.[4]

1. In the South, this came to be known as the one-drop rule, meaning that a single drop of "Black blood" makes one Black.
2. It is also called the one-Black ancestor rule.
3. The *hypo-descent* rule is the name given by anthropologists, at term wherein racially mixed people are assigned the status of their subordinate group.[5] This definition emerged from the American South to become a national definition, generally accepted by Blacks and Whites.[6]

Of course, there has been a great deal of litigation questioning these definitions, for example, *Plessy v. Ferguson* (163 US 537). Homer Plessy was the plaintiff in the 1896 precedent-setting separate-but-equal case. The case challenged the Jim Crow statute that required racially segregated seating on trains in interstate commerce in Louisiana. The U.S. Supreme Court quickly dispensed with Plessy's contention that because he as only one-eighth negro and could pass as White, he was entitled to ride in the seats reserved for Whites. The Supreme Court took "Judicial Notice" of what it assumed to be common community knowledge—that a negro or Black is any person with any African ancestry, in other words, the one-drop rule.

THE CASE OF SUSIE GUILLORY PHIPPS

Mrs. Susie Phipps had been denied a passport because she had checked "White" on her application as her color, although her birth certificate designated her race as "colored." The midwife reported her race according to the family's community standing. Mrs. Phipps claimed she was "shocked" that this classification was listed since she had always "thought she was white, had lived as white and twice married someone of the white race" (Susie Phipps, 470 So. 2d 369, 1970 Lawsuit La. Rev. Stat 42.267).

The Court of Appeals upheld the district court's decision saying no one can change the racial designation of his or her parents or anyone else's (Susie Phipps, 470 So. 2d 369, 1970 Lawsuit La. Rev. Stat 42.267). A preponderance of the evidence clearly showed Guillory's parents were colored.

A 1970 lawsuit said Phipps was 256/100 Black. The Louisiana legislature revised its law.[7] They began to define as "Black" someone with more than 1/32 Black ancestry (Susie Phipps, 470 So. 2d 369, 1970La. Rev. Stat. 42:267). The state abolished its 1/32 rule in 1983 (Susie Phipps, 470 So. 2d 369, Lawsuit La. Rev. Stat 42.267).

Back Story: Susie Guillory Phipps

In 1770 a (White) French planter named Jean Gregoire Guillory took his wife's (Black) slave Margarita as his mistress.[8] More than two centuries later, their great, great, great, great granddaughter, Susie Guillory Phipps, unsuccessfully asked courts to change the classification on her birth certificate from colored to White.[9] Apparently, the one-drop rule has some teeth and is very deeply rooted in our society.

Artistry and Race: Adrian Piper's Work on Identity

Hundreds of years later, conceptual artist, philosopher, and writer Adrian Piper has hewn her art around racial identity. Piper, who went to prep school and "ivory league" colleges, uses her formidable wit and analytic skills to bring racial stereotyping to the attention of Americans. Piper is Black, yet her skin is so fair and her physical features so classically European that she is frequently challenged by both Black and White cultures concerning her identity. Many people seem to challenge her assertion of blackness, digging for an ulterior motive. Piper states that she is simply proud to be Black. While some of her ancestors have long since melted into White society, her branch of the family is happy to be Black Americans.

In many ways, Piper is a role model for biracial, triracial, and light-skinned Blacks. She is unflinching in her examination of her family, her *self*, and the reactions to both in our society. Influenced by conceptual artists, minimalism, performance, the "art as life" movement, and the philosophy of Kant, Piper encourages viewers to transcend subconscious assessments of racial identity and urges them, sometimes through embarrassing confrontations, to change racist attitudes.

In the article "Passing for White, Passing for Black," in *Transition* (Issue 58, 1992), Piper recounts the pain incurred when a distinguished professor said, "Ms. Piper, you're about as Black as I am." She calls the accusation typical but admits that more often it comes from Blacks. Her family was one of the remaining middle-class, light-skinned Black families left in Harlem when she was growing up, as the others had moved to the suburbs. The remaining people were working class according to Piper. They called her "pale-face" or "Clorox baby" quite regularly. She recounts many painful memories incurred at the hand of her people and reports how demoralizing and alienating the exchanges made her feel. She uses words like *humiliation, betrayal, identity tests,* and *anger* frequently, in describing how her Black neighbors in Harlem treated her and how the antagonistic relationships made her feel.

At times Piper seems to feel guilty, that she is not darker skinned, but as an intellectual, she realizes this is a futile and demoralizing emotion. She reports the desire to become more detached, to forgive, to allow the freedom to feel helpless, though exaggerated fantasies of aggressors (White or Black) diminish their own responsibility to be humane toward others. Rejection seems to have toughened her attitude toward upper-class Whites and working-class Blacks. While she realizes that historically light-skinned Blacks have received preferential treatment, better jobs, and a higher education, she is firmly grounded in the here and now. Indeed, Piper has found that she thrives in the tan area, where character, personality, and deeds outweigh appearance and geographic origin. Her armor of self-worth is strengthened by calmly challenging the conventional thoughts of others; this is reinforced by her commitment to family and personal history.

Following are three other stories regarding identity, discovery, and a sense of well-being that comes from the successful merger of what is inside and out—when we pass for what we are—complex human beings.

MIXED HERITAGE—THE JUMBLE THAT WE ARE

An interview with Roberta Estes:

As a child, I vividly remember coming home from a powwow when I was 4 or 5 with my father and my mother furiously ripping the braids and braid ties from my hair. Her unusual reaction frightened me, and she would never tell me why she was so angry with my father.

I loved the powwow, the music, the dancing, even the smell . . . everything. To me, through my 5 year old eyes, it was the essence of happiness. I was too young to understand that the powwow was illegal in the 1950s, branded as a "religious event", and my mother did not want anyone to know that I was of mixed race.

It wasn't my mother's fault. She wanted the best opportunities for me, just like all mothers do, and I could clearly physically pass for white. However, as an exuberant 5 year old who now owned a beautiful fringed leather coat, a wonderful beaded belt and some braid wraps, I was extremely proud of my Native American heritage. Never had I felt more at home anyplace.

When I started school, in first grade, as we didn't have kindergarten or preschool then, I proudly announced that I was Indian. The teacher called my mother who had a chat with me and told me I should never tell anyone that secret again. I asked why, and she explained that white people didn't like colored people, and I was white, so I shouldn't say I was Indian. Even then, the logic escaped me, but I complied, most of the time.

The town where I grew up was segregated. The white people lived on one side of town and the black on the other and everyone knew where the dividing line was. Sometimes there was some intermixing a block or so in either direction, which is where we lived, on the white side, but not much. In the early 1960s, when I was 7 or 8, a new sign was erected outside our house. Normally it would be a "no parking" sign, but this one was different. My Mom seemed startled and shaken by it, and then she took me outside to see it. We stood in front of it and she asked if I could read the words. I slowly sounded them out one at a time, "colored", "people", "not", "allowed". She looked at me and said, "That is why you can never, ever tell anyone again that you are Indian." My father had just died, and the thought of losing my home because I was Indian, or colored, terrified me. I came to understand that if you weren't white, you were colored. Standing there, that day, I put my Indian heritage away someplace safe, and became as white as I could be.

However, the questions didn't stop. "Where are you from?" was normally the question asked. People would guess Morocco, Spain, Mexico, especially people who hadn't seen my mother who was of German origin. I just laughed and as a teenager, I loved the mystique I could invoke. But I knew, or at least I thought I knew, my secret.

My Native American heritage never left me. I read about the culture and longed for that connection I felt at the powwow so many years ago. When I entered college, I was told that I might be able to qualify for a scholarship. I discovered at that point, that the government regulated who was and was not an Indian, as there were a few left after their genocide attempt called the "Trail of Tears" was not wholly successful, and that the Cherokee tribe didn't want me either. I was too Indian for polite white society, which I lived in, but never fit, and not Indian enough for anyone else. I found it incomprehensive that I had been robbed of my heritage by both sides, and I began to grow angry, vowing to remedy that loss.

The year my daughter was born, 1978, is also the year that the American Indian Religious Freedom Act was passed, finally permitting powwows, sweat lodges and other spiritual events in addition to speaking the native tongue again. Sadly, much of the culture had already been lost.

I had, by this time, embraced my Native heritage in whatever ways that I could, without leadership or mentoring of any tribe. 1978 was also the year I would begin my three decade genealogical adventure, quite by accident. Although segregation officially ended in 1965, employment discrimination against women was still widely practiced and accepted in 1978, and I lost my job when I became pregnant. My employer informed me that he was doing me a favor because I would need to spend more time at home.

Unable to find a job during my pregnancy, I went back to college and also decided to find out something about my father's family. Both actions would forever change the course of my life. After my father's death, we had little contact with my father's family who lived three states away, and eventually, no contact at all. I picked up the phone and made a call to an Estes in Claiborne County, Tennessee . . . and as they say, one thing led to another.

I found a half-sister, and eventually, a half-brother, and countless cousins who I never knew existed. And they too were dark like me. I had found my way home to the magnificent hills and hollers of the Cumberland Gap area of Appalachia.

In the 1990s, on one of my annual journeys "home" to Appalachia, my old southern auntie finally took me into her confidence, knowing her days were numbered and one day leaned over, and even though we were alone, whispered behind her hand "we're Black Dutch, you know." Black Dutch? What is Black Dutch?

Black Dutch, it turns out, is a local (originally pejorative) term for Melungeon, a small group of tri-racial settlers who staked out their claims in the most remote mountainous areas of what would become Claiborne and Hawkins County, Tennessee in the late 1700s and very early 1800s. They, like the Scotch-Irish settlers, were very clannish and kept mostly to themselves, often intermarrying. And they were dark. They were rumored to be part Indian and part Black, although they claimed for decades to be of Portuguese ancestry. How much of that claim was to avoid the devastating southern segregation laws is unknown.

Today, DNA testing is underway along with intense historical research to determine, if possible, the genesis of the group of people who came to be known as Melungeons in Appalachia. Preliminary results do include DNA of African and Indo-European ancestry, although much more testing is needed for a comprehensive analysis.

I struggled a bit to internalize Black Dutch, and set about another journey of research and discovery, not yet complete today, that would ultimately land me a decade later smack dab in the middle of DNA analysis. I'm surely glad I went back to college when I did.

As the millennium turned, many questions about my heritage remained. Stories surfaced about Lazarus Estes who would not let his wife, Elizabeth, file for her Head Rights because he did not want anyone to know she was Indian, although her brothers let the cat out of the bag it seems. Secrets were whispered about ancestors hiding in the hills and caves instead of marching on the Trail of Tears, but maddeningly, no names were ever attached to these rich stories. I would find that Lazarus's father walked to Texas, much later, and when I visited after I finished retracing the Trail of Tears in 2006, I would discover that he lived in Oklahoma on Choctaw lands. My family continued to mystify me, and I desperately wanted to be able to unveil the mists that still surrounded my heritage that so stubbornly refused to yield its secrets.

In 2001, I discovered the infant science of DNA testing for genealogy. Initially, only the female maternal line could be tested, but in 2002, the paternal Y chromosome testing became available. Using these two tests, one could determine whether or not the paternal male line or the maternal female lines, only, were of Indo-European, African, Native American, or Asian ancestry. My Mother's maternal line was German, and I did not have a Y chromosome, being female, so I had to find a surrogate Estes male to test. Not surprisingly, the Estes line is from

England and does not carry the genetics of Africans or Native Americans in the Y chromosome itself.

However, these two tests only represent 2 of my many ancestral lines as you look at my pedigree chart, and my native ancestry clearly sprung from my other ancestors. At 5 generations back, my 32 ancestral lines were born about 1800. Any or all 32 of those grandparents, except for the Estes male represented by the Y line DNA test and the maternal grandmother represented by my mitochondrial DNA, could be Native. However, DNA testing was still in its infancy and not well known or accepted. Cousins who I asked to test as representative of those other lines were skeptical at best, when they could be located at all.

In 2003, a new kind of DNA test became available that tested specific locations in the balance of your DNA, which is most of what we carry, and it compared the results to population genetics result patterns from various parts of the world with the goal of providing you with an ethnic mix. This procedure is patented, so we know very little about the test itself or how the results are calculated, but as time and technology has evolved, the results seem to make better sense. The results were reported as statistically derived percentages and represented 4 categories, Indo-European, African, Asian and Native American. In this country, the Asian and Native American should generally be interpreted as a combined Native American score, given that the ancient ancestry of the Native American's is Asian.

My test results arrived by e-mail, and I sat staring at the little envelope on my screen before I clicked to open. It seemed that the truth of my heritage lay before me in a techno-Pandora's box and once I clicked, I could never unclick. Should I click? What if the results were that I was not Native American, a culture I had so strongly embraced and identified with since I was a small child? With the answer so close, I suddenly shied away from the answer to a half century of searching. It seemed such a mundane way to receive such a historic answer. Shouldn't there be fireworks and a drum roll? I closed my eyes, and clicked.

When I opened my eyes, I was quite surprised. Yes indeed. I expected, based on what I knew genealogically, to carry only a small percentage of Native American DNA and the balance Indo-European. Instead, I carried some of all 4 groups, with the combined Native score reaching more than 25% and African in the small percentage I expected to carry of Native American. Retrospectively, this does not surprise me, as I knew that physical features typically don't manifest themselves unless the individual has 25% or more of a particular ethnicity.

The African was a complete surprise to me. I began to analyze both historical documents and family photos with a different eye. Where did the Native and African heritage come from? Clearly, with this much non-white admixture, it had to be from more than one ancestral line, or I would clearly know which of my grandparents, who each contributed approximately 25% of their genes to me, was Native. With my Mother's German heritage, it also appeared clear that this admixture was on my father's side of that pedigree chart, reducing the number of candidates from 30 to 15.

At this point, given that we inherit half of our genes from each parent, I desperately wanted to test both of my parents. My mother was still living, but my father would have had to be exhumed for the test. I tried unsuccessfully to have DNA extracted from his hair and a postage stamp. Discovering that exhumation was a long and involved legal jungle, I opted to test Mother with the assumption that she would be 100% Indo-European.

Never assume. My mother had a whopping 9% combined score between Native American (2%) and Asian (7%). I wasn't stunned, I was dumbfounded. Where did this come from? Very low numbers can sometimes be statistical noise, but when I asked my mother about this, she graced me with the information that she was not surprised, because of the oral history of her one non-Germanic ancestor, Anthony Lore, who was French and found in Vermont, then Pennsylvania. He did indeed have a very secretive and checquered life, but Native American? How could that ever be?

When interpreting non-American results, one cannot combine the Asian and Native American quite so readily. The Huns invaded Germany, and several of my Mother's ancestral lines were from the exact location of the Hunnic invasions and resulting settlement. Her mitochondrial DNA is also of Middle Eastern descent, possibly Jewish, confirming interaction with the peoples who could easily carry Asiatic DNA.

However, the Native American portion indicates that she too could have a small portion of Native heritage, suspected by her but completely unknown to me, and that it was 2–9%, it would likely be about 4–5 generations back in time. This equates to the parents or grandparents of Anthony Lore, born 1806 in Canada.

Another 5 years would pass before one single word at the right time and place would unlock the mystery of my mother's Native heritage, although it still sounds odd to voice those words together. A researcher working on the Lost Colony DNA project would comment about their ancestors in Vermont, which is where my mother's Lore ancestor was found earliest, bordering Canada. He referred me to an individual who had indexed many documents, and she referred me to Blairfindie, a small village in the middle of a small Acadian settlement in Canada between Montreal and the Vermont border. In Blairfindie, I found an Anthony Lord, also spelled Lore, and others of this same family with names that matched he children of my Anthony Lore. This isn't the ancestral family, but I'm close, and perhaps even more important, we discovered that the family is Acadian.

The Acadian's frequently intermarried with the Mi'kmaq (Micmac) before and during the 1755 Removal when those that survived did so in the woods or were murdered or deported. This certainly potentially explains mother's Native American admixture.

My simple phone call of 30 years ago launched me on the journey of thousands of miles and 3 continents to find ancestors I never knew existed. I am truly a citizen of the earth, a mutt, a true Heinz 57. I am proud of all of my ancestors, black, white, red and yellow, for their tenacity in the face of adversity, but I am especially proud to be able to resurrect my ancestors and ancestresses of color individually from the grave, beyond the veil of prejudice and hypocrisy.[10]

PASSING FOR WHITE—PASSING FOR BLACK

Whereas Roberta's family was quite eager to pass as pure White, another interviewee, California graduate student, Shanel speaks of finding out that perhaps folks in her family were passing for Black, for reasons that remain as baffling as the people themselves.

The Story of Szmeralda

Like many African Americans in this country I know that technically I am multiracial (African, Native American, and European). West African, English/Irish, possibly Scottish if we're looking at surnames, Creek and Choctaw. Though my experience in this world is as a Black woman and while it's romantic and fashionable to be multiracial these days, it is as a Black woman that I move in the world, am seen, and identify.

My family is from the South East, Louisiana, Mississippi, Alabama, Tennessee. We all come in various shades of browns, reds, yellows, hell some of us could pass for White. Some of us have wavy rusty hair and green eyes, others tight curled black hair and brown eyes, but we're all Black.

When I got my DNA results I was shocked, confused, and pretty upset. I could not find my West African ancestry. The African countries that did show up in my results were North African-Moroccan, some Egyptian and they were not high on the list of results. Most of my DNA matches were in Eastern Europe a group of people in Romania called the Csango who trace their ancestry back to Hungarians. Next was Bosnia, then Russia then Basque Spain. I also had high DNA matches in Poland, Italy, Brazil, and Australia. I did not have a problem with my European matches, I was upset that I could not find my West African matches when I am a Black American. My first thought was, "Well damn, if I got'ta have White all up in my DNA, then I need to at least be getting some of that White privilege. I should print this out so the next time I'm experiencing racism I can hold up my White folks papers." (That's a lil' joke, so laugh).

The strangest thing is, on an intuitive level, I was aware of my connection to these places. The first time I got on an airplane, I flew to Hungary to visit a friend. When I got there, the people felt very familiar to me (even though on the streets of Budapest experienced some racism). I took day trips to Romania and Poland, felt confusing nostalgia, playful curiosity, a dash of pain, a splash of sadness. I've always had a strange yearning to go to Russia, never really knowing why other than finding the onion top buildings beautiful and intriguing. When I visited Italy at 17 I fell in love immediately and believed it to possibly be my true home. In the goddess-centered spirituality I practice, my goddess-given name is Szmeralda (pronounced Esmeralda) in Spanish, but I purposely spelled it the way I thought it would be spelled if it were written the Eastern European way. It's all so strange but interesting to have my DNA results come out this way when I am so brown and obviously African American.

In my family there is a story about my great grandmother's people. It is said that one day they just showed up.

"They just showed up in Mississippi where the rest of us had been living all the time and knew each other. I tell you they came from out of no where. One day they wasn't there and the next day they was, and there was a bunch of 'em, I tell you they just popped up like weeds. And they were very strange. They had dark-dark skin and thick straight black hair, the prettiest hair you ever see. They would wash it the water on the rocks and then just lay out there and let it dry like that. They looked like Mexicans or something."

This story is told by the oldest living person in my family. Many in the family assume that these people were Native Americans but are confused about why folks wouldn't have recognize as "Indians" since Indians had been around Black folks in the South forever . . .

When I did the research I found that all of the countries that I had high DNA matches in were all places that had significantly high populations of Romany people. I was surprised (kind'a). Ironically, I've been calling myself a Black Gypsy for as long as I can remember. I have been called this by people who have not known that I've called myself this. I had another DNA test that showed high matches with the Romany people (also known as Gypsies) and was verified. Still when it comes down to it, for me it's all about experience and culture which means, while I am technically multiracial, really, I'm a Black American woman.[11]

TALES FROM INSIDE THE MELTING POT

Having done plenty of ruminations and study on my ancestry and heritage recently through findings by genealogy and DNA tests, these are my thoughts describing my discoveries and feelings about finding out that perhaps I wasn't the kind of Black, White, or Indian person I thought I was since the geography and proportions varied so greatly from what I thought I had known. The swirling questions remain for me, and they might come up for you when you do in-depth testing and genealogy—what could this all mean to the person that you are and have become? What does it truly mean to your identity?

Like most African Americans from the southeast coast of the United States, I thought I knew my ethnic heritage. We have a lengthy heritage for the most part, entwined for better or worse, with the stodgy old planter culture of colonial America. So, some of us may have Irish, English, German, or Scottish names like me, including Hurst, Gillespie, Vaughan, Daniel, Hunt, and Callahan, depending on the geographic locale, as well as plenty of monikers from elsewhere across Europe.

Some of us mixed right into Native American communities becoming Seminole, Creek, and Lumbee—a beautiful, undeniably triracial people. As all three stories illustrate, we assume we know our heritage, and by all indications it is West African with some English/Irish and Native American, but before I put the period there, that has come to mean African American, right? Well, maybe not.

I have been writing this book about mixed race for quite some time, mixed raced, people called triracial and biracial in America. Along the way, I started paying closer attention to DNA ancestry tests, and through paying attention, I started to hear diverse conversations. The one that stuck in my mind, in my craw actually, was the one where people defined culturally as "White" had tests coming back with smidgens of sub-Saharan African (SSA). These people would then converse online chatting more freely in the virtual world than perhaps they do in the real world, about whether or not they had thick lips, frizzy hair, and well . . . a big butt. Some would write in to these different Web sites with riotous indignation: These tests are flawed, they'd assert. I'm pure White, white as a lily; all my heritage traces back to merry old England. I've got the paper work to prove it! Okay, so I paraphrase, but only to make the point of what I was reading.

Here, at my writer's desk, I was relatively smug. I already knew and accepted that I was mixed. The typical, dare I say, all-American mix, Black, White, and Red. End of story . . . but not quite. I kept reading those chats. It became almost compulsive must-read entertainment. I found African American–orientated Web sites with pissed off people, too—ones where folks couldn't find their haplogroup to be sub-Saharan African. If you're not up on all this lingo, if you can't find your haplogroup in the place you feel is your origin—well, someone has some 'splaining to do or you have to do some research on your own. These people who could not find their haplogroups in typical sub-Saharan African lineage, for example the "L" group, were pissed with a capital *P*.

Still at my writer's chair, now something funny began to percolate. Some White folks, perhaps they were not White but light-skinned Blacks passing for White—hence the obvious "Black" phenotypes cropping up, for example, deeply tanned skin, thicker lips, broad noses . . . the "big ass" mentioned in a confidentially toned blog. Hmmm, oh well, I thought, serves them right. We knew many of us (African Americans) were mixed on the plantations, good to see the stirring of the stewpot went both ways.

But I got up out of this comfy writer's chair. I started feeling my way in society with blinders off and also remembering how so many different cultures embraced me as one of their own. I mean far out people to the tightly fixed notion that most of us African Americans hold dear, like Aborigines, South East Asians and Indians, Balkan people, and Mediterranean as well as Arabic speakers. Curiosity got the best of me. I had one test by National Geographic through the Genographic Project. Not satisfied simply knowing my haplotype was L1, I wanted percentages, so I went for another test (DNA by Ancestry) where I clearly saw the ratios of my sub-Saharan African, Indo-European, and Native American extractions. But what do percentages tell you unless you know what those percentages consist of? So I had even more specific tests by DNA Tribes and Family Tree DNA—six in all, and sad to say, I'm not finished yet.

Now, I must admit I was frustrated as everyone else when the results received were not those anticipated. I found scant Native American, though my great-great grandmother was said to be Cherokee. Nothing from the British Isles, though my great grandfather was said to be British, and most shocking of all, my African profile was completely skewed. Rather than the West African heritage showing up prominent as expected, I was awash in South African of every which type. Moreover, I have even more eastern African than western and some northern thrown in there, even suspected Angolan pygmy.

OK, almost as a joke . . . yes, it must be a karmic joke, the day after St. Patrick's, my sixth result came rolling in over the Internet transom as a PDF file. And on the first page of results after my known hefty dose of South African, Caribbean, and African American was a plausible ratio from Ireland, which none of the previous tests showed. But it was too late to bust out the Emerald Green—the day was over, LOL.

I am that mixing pot I hear about less and less. No wonder different types of people respond to me as though I am one of their own; in some ways, I am. Very African—no surprise there. The South African makes me proud as does the affiliation with nomadic north Africans such as the Berbers because they have had a lot thrown at them and they keep going. In terms of Africa, I am mostly of the south and southeast with some western and northern and that arrangement is indeed a surprise and wonderful. What better gift that to find I am continental African?

Today's refinements continued to show an appreciable Arabic and Mesopotamian of the Turkish type. I must say, though, who those or that relative was I am totally uncertain. It is a delicious mystery. There was Sicilian this time—huh?—some Balkan and nomadic Mongolian . . . more scratches of the head, and alas the results were awash in Spanish and Portuguese waters—this evident connection is incontrovertible.

What I love about these tests is I could spin about in the mirror, looking for stereotypes of one type or another, maybe reflect on my wide but flat ass, but instead I've gone to the history books hitting them very hard. I see the South African's were taken over for a time by Arabic speakers as well as the Portuguese. I see through history books that ethnicity is kind of a joke, and invasions blurred geographic boundaries and the people within, stirring the pot and stirring the pot and stirring the pot some more until a South African with Italian/Spanish/Portuguese blood, layered over with Moroccan/Arab/Turkish, some Balkan, and even smidgens of India and Samoa is possible.

I think these DNA tests are beautiful and spiritually opening, though far from perfected. They verify that we are a blended folk and that we should respect that from within ourselves and by all means should respect other cultures. Who knows—perhaps they are our own?

These days culture seems a lot more tangible than race, so I must return to my writer's chair continuing this *Light, Bright, and Damn Near White* story, hopefully with fresh and innovative notions.

At the end of the twentieth century, major changes that have recently occurred in American society offer hope for the realization of better race relations in the twenty-first century. These include the dynamic force of generational replacement, the shifting of the demographic landscape, the growth of a strong Black middle class, the enlistment of large numbers of racial minorities in the U.S. military, and the gradual erosion of racial boundaries resulting from increasing rates of interracial marriages and transracial adoptions. These changes make it difficult to maintain the status quo in relation to race.

Generational replacement and demographic changes weaken the foundations on which race is socially constructed, each successive generation of

Americans becomes more tolerant and supportive of racial integration and equality. Greater access to education, increased interaction among individuals from different racial backgrounds, and society's growing intolerance of racist attitudes and behaviors consolidate this trend. The influx of immigrants also helps weaken racial boundaries by complicating the concept of race and racial categorization.

—Richard J. Payne[12]

There is so much ignorance, stereotyping and shame preventing us from understanding who we really are and how we are related to one another. On average, there is .02 percent difference between any two randomly selected people on the face of the earth. Of that diversity, 85 percent will be found within any local group of people. More than half (9%) of the remaining 15 percent will be represented by the difference between ethnic and linguistic groups within a given race. Only 6 percent represents differences between the races (6% of 0.2%). In other words, race amounts for a minuscule 0.012 percent difference in our genetic material.[13]

The Human Genome Project has beautifully documented the genetic commonalities that exist in all humans, yet many people have still not integrated this information into their consciousness. It is my hope as a healer that this and the following chapters will be a cultural gift. Using personal stories, statistics, and a historical backdrop, I am hoping to demonstrate clearly and concisely the numerous possibilities and richness within triracial, biracial, multicultural, or intercultural heritage—a wealth that resides within us all.

NOTES

1. Danzy Stanza, "The Mulatto Millennium," in *Half and Half: Writers on Growing up Biracial and Bicultural,* ed. Claudine Chiawei O'Hearn (New York: Pantheon Books, 1998), 15.

2. Ibid., 22–27.

3. John Langston Gwaltney, *Drylongso: A Self Portrait of Black America* (New York: Vintage Books, 1980), 96.

4. Gunnar Myrdal, *An American Dilemma: The Negro Problem and Modern Democracy,* (New York: HaperCollins, 1944), 113–18.

5. Harris Melvin, *56 Patterns of Race in the Americas* (New York: W. W. Norton, 1964), 56.

6. Joseph M. Bahr, Bruce A. Chadwick, and Joseph H. Strauss, *American Ethnicity* (Lexington, MA: DC, Heath and Company, 1979): 27–28.

7. Calvin Trillin, "American Chronicles: Black and White," *New Yorker,* April 14, 1986, 77.

8. Peter F. Model, "Apartheid in the Bayou," *Perspectives: The Civil Rights Quarterly* 15 (Winter-Spring, 1998): 3–4.

9. Ibid., 62–78.

10. Written transcript provided with permission by Roberta Estes.

11. Written transcript interview provided with permission by Szmeralda Shanel Jackson.

12. Richard J. Payne, *Getting Beyond Race: The Changing American Culture* (Boulder, CO: Westview Press, 1998), 193.

13. Paul Hoffman, "The Science of Race," *Discover* 15 (1994): 4.

CHAPTER 3

Tan Territory: Separating Fact, Fiction, and Fantasy

Who are you? Where did you come from? Why are you here?

These are three fundamental questions to the human condition, and they ask us to identify ourselves using place of origin which typically signifies ethnicity. While in the United States these questions may come in candy-colored codes, in the outback of Australia, I was met with these questions head-on, in broken English, with a serious curiosity I had not anticipated. "I'm Stephanie," I simply wanted to say, "and this is my family," but I knew it wasn't the appropriate response. Often in Australia, living among the Aborigines, I was also asked what clan and moiety I was from, and even by White Australians, what was my ancestral connection to the Aboriginal and Torres Strait Islander People that had brought me down under? I'm interested in their culture, I was thinking on the one hand, yet on the other hand, I never considered for a second that I could be related to Aboriginal or Torres Strait Islander People. Years later, through DNA testing, I found out I am . . . scratch of the head.

Who are you? Where did you come from? Why are you here? How do you relate genetically to those around you?

Do you ever ask yourself those questions? Well, when you are biracial, intercultural, interracial, triracial, or multiracial, and most of you are, whether you admit it or not, these questions are at the core of your daily activities.

INTRODUCTION TO THE TAN TERRITORIES

I have known of the tan world since I was a child, growing up with two different sides of the family, having one biracial grandparent each. I use to think my known grandparents alone defined me culturally, but that doesn't begin to describe the full story. Our genetic lines do not begin or end with grandparents. As I've done intensive genealogy studies and a number of DNA tests, I have found that there have been multiple admixtures in my line, in part due to the fact that if you had to summarize "my people," they are a seafaring, coastal people. When you live at the shore, there is no doubt that there will be contact with others from far and wide.

Once more, I want to reiterate the importance of questioning identity.

> Who are you? Where did you come from? Why are you where you are? How do you relate genetically and culturally to those around you?

Even if you are one to have a phenotype that seems to define you as monoracial, step out of the mask and deal with these questions. It may open a rich, Pandora's box of possibilities, interactions, and meaningful interchanges with what you once thought of as "others."

IS THERE A BOX FOR YOU?

Your birth family, blood relatives if you will, are a reliable mirror for your racial and ethnic composition. What I saw at our family get-togethers was a phenomenological, kaleidoscopic vision of diversity. These people were not meant to be one-box checkers; hardly anyone seemed monoracial.

From grade school onward, I challenged the notion of monoracialism. I can remember being given a questionnaire in grammar school about my racial identification. Almost always, I would check as many boxes as I understood or suspected myself to be; often none were left blank. I can see, them now, these forms, floating in my mind's eye, piled up in some kind of cemetery for improperly filed out forms. I know now, especially during the 1960s and 1970s when I was filling out these census-type questionnaires, the *raison d'etre* was to determine whether students of Alloway Township's school system were Black or White. We were—all that and much more.

However, the box constructors were busy at work as early as 1879, when in *Principia of Ethnology: The Origins of Races and Color,* Martin R. Delany states:

> That it may be indelibly fixed on every mind, we place on record the fact, that the races as such, especially black and white are indestructible—that miscegenation as it is popularly understood—the running out of two races, or several into a new race cannot take place.[1]

By the early 1900s, there is a statement made that more closely reflects reality.

So arbitrary a method of placing populations in racial categories seems to me to be obviously unsound when one considers the amount of mixture which all contemporary peoples represent. Of course, one may broadly categorize but this is usually more or less self-evident classification.[2]

According to Maria P. P. Root, the sorts of questions I am asking arise in the context of a country that has held particular views of race:

A country that has subscribed to race as an immutable construct, perceived itself as White, and been dedicated to preserving racial lines. Thus such questions of race and identity can only precipitate a full-scale 'identity crisis' that this country is ill-equipped to resolve.

She goes further to state:

The "racial ecology" is complex in a phenotypically heterogeneous society that has imbued physical differences with significant meaning in a convention that benefits selective segments of society. At a personal level, race is very much in the eye of the beholder; at a political level, race is in the service of economic and social privilege. Ethnic identity is relevant only in an ethnically heterogeneous environment.[3]

To paraphrase Root's work further: Linear models of social relationships have provided the basis for many social and psychological notions about racially mixed people. The monoracial and monocultural bias of these notions and theories is evident in the construction of assimilation and aculturalization models. Many of the earlier theories addressing identity issues for people of mixed ancestry perform a disservice. The theories, like our racial classification system, are filled with dichotomous or bipolar schemes which only serve to marginalize the overall status of racially, culturally or ethnically blended individuals.[4]

The recent consideration of a multiracial precept presents the possibility that a person can have simultaneous memberships and multiple classifications that deconstruct marginality and multidimensional models of identity. It further shows phenotype, genotype and ethnicity do not necessarily coincide with or reliably predict identity.[5]

WHERE DOES TAN FIT IN THE AMERICAN RACIAL RAINBOW?

Several of my book titles are based on old chants that I heard when growing up. "Sticks, Stones, Roots, and Bones," for example, stuck in my mind because when we moved to the country, often I was called nigger. It was "nigger this, nigger that . . . " or just the chant "nigger, nigger, nigger." I wore a dense cloak daily on my way to school, not just the sort of woolen one that was popular during those days, but that phrase, "Sticks and stones will break my bones but names will never hurt me." I was rooted in a decent, though like a tree, not unshakable sense of self, that went far beyond the derogatory terms flung toward me.

At that time during the 1960s and 1970s, it was common to hear the chant "Light, Bright, Damned Near White" at people who were obviously of mixed heritage. The blunt ethnic-cultural description "Black" did a fine job of eradicating the usage of terms *quadroon, octoroon,* and *mulatto,* which had become divisive. Yet such a blanket term as *Black* could never erase the complexity of mixed-race heritage. In South America, mestees and mestizos are a blended racial group with a distinctive identity shaped by a confluence of cultural influences. Apart from anthropologists and other scholars, few Americans readily use those particular terms when discussing multiracial or multicultural groups.

In the second half of the twentieth century, a concerted effort was made in North America to characterize people who were often of mixed heritage as simply White or Black. According to Itaberi Njeri:

> As one of the oldest and largest populations of mixed ancestry in the United States and the most politically influential, African Americans in the debate over multiracial identity have an opportunity to force an expanded definition of community for ourselves and the nation. But at the national level, African American politicians have been conspicuously absent from the debate, even though their constituencies have a huge stake in a positive outcome.[6]

Some individuals of mixed heritage readily adopt the crisp, White or Black racial tags, even though Blacks in particular are not in any way an old-fashioned race in the biological sense.[7] Lamely, many advocates for the multiracial category listing argue that since African Americans, and by the way White Americans, see themselves as monoracial, it would be presumptuous to challenge their self-identification.[8] A new generation of tan people seek accurate definitions of their complex identity. For these people, checking the "other" box on an application or census is not an option, as it excludes segments of their ancestral heritage—often a parent or grandparents.

PERSONAL INSIGHTS

Like many other Americans, I always knew that I was African, Native American, and European by bloodlines, but knew I was Black in the eyes of America. As an artist and writer, I have been candid and dogged in my exploration of race. I know that I am a mélange of many cultures, though I identify culturally and racially with being Black while recognizing strong Native American and European influence.

When I began writing my memoir *A Walkabout Home*, I wanted to be quite candid about my ethnicity, after all, my entire memoir is an exploration of identity. My memoir explores physical, spiritual, and metaphysical being. Through my grandmother and her sisters, I heard strange names like Red Bone, Guinea, and Moor—silently, I wondered if they were talking about themselves. Then, too, Grandma frequently mentioned that when she was in New England people thought she was of Portuguese descent. Quite naturally, I wanted to know if I were indeed a "Red Bone," a cultural group name Black folks felt comfortable assigning based on appearance, or if my family were descendants of the "Guineas." Looking through my family photographs, I notice an array of skin colors from black to white, with mostly tan families in between. According to family legend, several groups opted out of Black society entirely, creating for themselves a mythic ancestry, living as White ethnics instead.

TOO LIGHT TO BE BLACK, TOO DARK TO BE WHITE—THE WAY OF MY PEOPLE

Pop, Ma's dad, had an interesting story and a peculiar way about him. He was born in 1890 on a plantation, the son of the English-Irish master and a mixed-race enslaved mother. While this is common family knowledge, it should be noted that such offspring raised as free children are an anomaly. I say he was peculiar because he was a true reflection of his father who was White, more so than his African-descended Mother. He never really saw himself as Black; nevertheless, he knew he wasn't White either. A proud colored "Negro"—still, though most of us had embraced the concept of blackness long ago. His manners had strong affinities toward the British Isles rather than sharing the casual impromptu nature of either White or Black American culture. Intercultural as well as interracial, he was proper to a fault: a real old-fashioned gentleman and philosophical to boot. He had a never-ending stockpile of proverbs and this is one of his few strong Africanisms.

Then there was Dad's part of the family. As if we were counting down to New Year, lil' brother and I were spellbound by an excruciating anticipation when we visited Dad's family, as we'd mark off the 17 or so exits of the New Jersey Turnpike and parkway that drew the lines between North and South Jersey. We headed to North Jersey or, more specifically, to East Orange. It wasn't the city itself that moved us. East Orange was experiencing the steep decline that has blighted many a Black neighborhood. There was dwindling police presence, with an increase in drug dealing, number running (street lottery), violent crime, and funeral homes. Still, we loved the place, not for what it was, but because it was our ancestral home. Almost all of our people on Dad's side of the family lived within a few miles of East Orange—Mom's as well.

My great grandmother was a laundress. To some folks' ears that may sound humble, almost shameful, but it was a decent, well-paying job for a woman of color during her times. It was not without its challenges either, as the clientele tended to be upper-class White people from suburban West Orange, Short Hills and Upper Montclair in North Jersey. Ironing and mending were her specialties. She was a reddish-brown-skinned woman with cottony soft hair and high cheek bones; her mother was part Native American. My father would recount memories of her strength, clarity, and wisdom; what a great cook she was, how very tough she was, but for us she was a warm, wise elder.

When we would arrive at Gran'ma's building, soon as she'd buzz us in, the blend of aromas told us that she'd been much too busy glazing the clove-and-maraschino-cherry-covered ham, watching over the bubbling macaroni and cheese casserole; chopping and then soaking the gritty collard, turnip, and mustard greens (she loved mixed greens); and buttering up the buttermilk rolls for church. Come to think of it, Great Grandma brought the church right over to her daughter's place with her, being that her religious work was never quite finished.

The incongruity wasn't limited to mother (Great-Grandma) and daughter (Grandma), the first holy and the later more interested in partying and fun after her hard days bustin' up the kids who taunted her and her fair-skinned, long-haired sisters, too light-skinned to even be called "yella," instead it was "Whitey Girls," "Crackers," and "Paddys." This, the daily chant, on their way to school from people of their own race, something we know today still exists, as colorism. Her rite of passage into adulthood led to days of washin' up after rich White folk as a live-in, not far off from the drudgery of slave days. Still, in the eyes of most, she was fortunate enough to have "good" steady work just like her mother it was on a comfortable estate, so she didn't complain. Come to think of it, she never complained. Clearly, she had no time for the notion of the *tragic mulatto.* Her ease with herself set the tone of all of our get-togethers. Her laughter was genuine—drawn deep—from the soul.

If I had to break Grandma down into bloodline fractions so popular during the days of old (Octoroon, Quadroon, Mulatto), I'd say she was one-quarter Bette Davis, one-quarter Billy Holiday, one-quarter Joan Crawford, one-quarter Alberta Hunter, and 100 percent Oya of Wind and Rain. As a child, I was never as at peace, as when I was snuggled up to Grandma, under her overstuffed down comforter. Her room smelled of mixture of lilacs and cedarwood. Tough, sweet and witty, she had long, silky, henna-reddened hair, with numerous shades of glorious red finger nail polishes and lipsticks, lined up in the bathroom to match. She embodied the wise woman: smart, seasoned, courageous, and sweet. A woman whose life came to a sharp edge—an edge she was very happy to bring you to the brink of, if you cared to listen.

My great grandmother's brother was also an eccentric, high-end domestic. He had taken to Irish and Scottish garb, and the last time I saw him he was in a wheel chair wearing tartan plaid and a fishermen's sweater.

In his younger years, he had been a butler, with all the attending airs to match.

When I was growing up, it was a rude awakening to move from north to south New Jersey. You would think an interstate move down the turnpike would only require a minor adjustment. However, we moved from an almost entirely Black enclave to a historically White, segregated small town. This was in the late 1960s. I had not heard "nigger" uttered, but in South Jersey, it was a tag line readily assigned, on playgrounds, in the classroom, and occasionally on the side of the road.

Among my own people, I remember at a very early age being called yellow, 'Rican, and red bone. Some of the girls said I had hair like a baby doll, and I rather liked that, as it didn't sound malicious, though, as they were also Black, it did highlight me as somehow being "other."

In short, I guess I am the descendant of three lines of "house niggers" granted position because of their mixed heritage. I see no need to compensate, feel shameful, or pay penance, especially since we also had plenty of lines of "'field hands" who worked the tobacco fields in my family as well. That is just how things were, and I cannot and will not turn my back on my ancestors or the opportunities I enjoy that result from the sweat of their labor or their cultural identity. I remain curious about the rainbow, particularly the history of tan America, which remains something of a mystery. I also seek out role models who can remain tough, united, and inspirational in the face of both racism and colorism.

My search for identity led me on a meandering trail of research. I learned how to trace race online. I felt that this offered some objectivity that my relatives might lack. I was able to identify my relationship to the triracial isolate groups, with certainty based on my ancestors' homeland, customs, and surnames. Separating fact from fiction can be tricky. Today, we can look at historical precedence, folklore, and geography to paint a fuller picture. Moreover, as we shall see at the conclusion of the book, a plethora of genetic tests and innovative genealogical tools as well as social networks provide answers and comfort, when once ambiguity or secrecy flourished.

OLD WORLD IN THE NEW WORLD: FACT, FICTION, AND FANTASY

Getting back to my grandmother and the Portuguese question touches on many fascinating elements of our history as Americans. Throughout early American history, the notion of being of Portuguese heritage was a rather common designation assigned to mixed-raced people, as was the idea of having a Moorish or Turkish background. In many ways, identification with a foreign "other," masked the possibility of domestic admixtures with exoticism, giving such individuals some immunity from segregation, humiliating laws, and social exclusion.

I have found a strong genetic connection between the Portuguese and my family exists, which points to repeated admixing probably as a result of my mother's family being of the Tsongan tribe, a tribe of southern Africans ruled for a time by the Portuguese. I was blown away when I found out this background, moreover that I had some Turkish, Moroccan, Arab, and quite a bit of Spanish. It didn't fit that oral stories I had heard or the history, as I viewed it at the time, of settlers, colonists, and explorers associated with the southeast coast of the United States—little did I know.

The Spanish settled and colonized much of the southern United States, particularly the Gulf States. Who is to say they limited themselves to those territories rather than moving on and upward toward Virginia and North Carolina? The Portuguese, Turkish, and Moors not only interacted with people of color in the United States, perhaps creating progeny of their own, but where heavily involved with Black communities in Africa and the Caribbean. There is a very real connection, as highlighted by a great deal of the Melungeon culture's DNA tests and genealogy, between the Portuguese, Spanish, Turkish, Moors, and longtime southern residents of the United States. Writing this book has been eye opening for me in that regard. I realize I had been quick to judge what could or could not be. For example, I thought the possibility of my having any Portuguese, Spanish, Turkish, Arab, Polynesian, or Aboriginal Australian blood would have to be some sort of fantasy I'd dreamed up. Thanks to DNA testing, I have found that I have connections to these groups and several others. I have also found my tribal affiliations in Africa—something many African Americans hunger for—yet even those tribes are at the opposite end of the map from where I thought I'd find my ancestry.

SEPARATING FACT FROM FICTION

For others, a connection to the Portuguese, Turkish, or Moors, whether factual or mythic, afforded opportunities that would have been denied to a triracial or biracial families with Black, White, and Indian heritage. Obviously, numerous Americans descend from the Portuguese, Turks, and Moors. For some mixed-raced people, though, the shroud afforded by a mythic ethnic identity enabled them to survive and prosper in early American society. No wonder my Grandma found the ethnicities assigned to her amusing, and yet in certain circumstances she was unwilling to deny such ancestry. This is the tightrope for social survival that many people walked.

Depending on the environment, the assumption of an Old World heritage proved useful to biracial and triracial Americans, as illuminated by court cases tried over a hundred years ago. Here are a few historical notes from a famous court case regarding the "Portuguese" (biracial) ambiguity as seen through the eyes of early Americans. The case was tried in Johnson County, Tennessee, in 1858. The documentation provides a glimpse into the way residents of the community readily embraced mixed families of purportedly foreign (Old World) origins, like the Perkins.

Joshua Perkins, born circa 1732 in Accomack County, Virginia, was the "Mulatto" son of a White woman.[9] He owned land in Robeson County, North Carolina, in 1761, moved to Liberty County, South Carolina, and in 1785 moved to what later became Washington County, Tennessee.[10] Succeeding generations of Perkins continued to marry either light-skinned Blacks or Whites of northern European descent, fading their African features. They were a prosperous family, owning a ferry, racehorses, and an iron ore mine. Members of this family ran the local schoolhouse and held official offices. Undercover, as an olive-skinned people with ties to Old World southern Europe, they reaped the benefits of societal acceptance. As the political winds changed abruptly, right before the Civil War in 1858, one of the Perkins was "accused" of being a Negro. He brought an unsuccessful lawsuit, accusing the defendant of slander.

Jacob F. Perkins, great-grandson of Joshua Perkins, brought an unsuccessful suit against one of his neighbors in the Circuit Court of Johnson County for slander because he called him a "free Negro."[11]

At least 50 people gave depositions or testified during his trial. Many of the deponents were from well-established families who had lived in North Carolina, South Carolina, or Tennessee for more than three generations. Only 16 of the elder witnesses testified that he was a "Negro," describing him as follows:

> Dark skinned man with sheep's wool and flat nose . . .[12]
>
> black man, hair nappy . . . Some called Jacob (his son) a Portuguese and some a negro.[13]
>
> Knew old Jock (Joshua) in North Carolina on Peedee . . . right black or nearly so. Hair kinky . . . like a common negro.[14]

However, several witnesses for Perkins testified that Joshua Perkins was something other than "Negro," and possibly Portuguese or Indian. They said little about his physical characteristics and those of his descendants. Instead, they argued that he could not have been a "Negro" because he was admired and trusted by the community. This raises an important issue that will be explored later, that Black is not only a racial trait but also comes to describe the character of an individual:

> dark skinned man . . . resembled an Indian more than a negro. He was generally called a Portuguese. *Living well . . . Kept company with everybody. Kept race horses and John Watson rode them.*[15]
>
> mixed blooded and not white. His wife fair skinned . . . *They had the same privileges.*[16]
>
> Hair bushy & long—not kinky. Associated with white people . . . *Associated with . . . the most respectable persons.* Some would call them negroes and some Portuguese.[17]

> He was known of the Portuguese race . . . *Four of his sons served in the Revolution . . . Jacob and George drafted against Indians . . . they came from and kept a ferry in South Carolina.*[18]
>
> *They kept company with decent white people and had many visitors.*[19]
>
> *I taught school at Perkins school house* . . . they were Portuguese . . . *associated white peoples, clerked at elections and voted and had all privileges.*[20]

The Perkins family live in the hazy tan area of the rainbow. There was a societal agreement about their identity that approached legendary status. Many of those who testified never even met the family but still felt certain of their identity. Rather than suspending racism and racial stereotype, the community adopted a myth of the Perkins' identity, allowing the status quo to be perpetuated. This was done by admitting mixed-race people into their society, as variants of their own European heritage.

> I was well acquainted with Jacob Perkins (a second generation Perkins). A yellow man—said to be Portuguese. They do not look like negroes. I have been about his house a great deal and nursed for his wife. She was a little yellow and called the same race. Had blue eyes and black hair. Was visited by white folks.[21]

A 77 year old, Daniel Stout, asserted, "never heard him called a negro. People in those days said nothing about such things."[22]

THE MELUNGEON, BLACK DUTCH AND "GYPSY"

I am not trying to suggest that White early-Americans were generally an open-minded people to anyone who seemed of European descent. There is plenty of scholarly and genetic debate regarding the absorption of undesirable European cultures into various Southern cultures in the United States. This adds further color to our discussion. In *The Black Dutch, German Gypsies or Chicanere and Their Relation to the Melungeon,* author Linda Griggs describes the Melungeon as "an olive complected, dark eyed, dark skinned people living in Appalachia."[23] While some Melungeon claim Portuguese heritage, this ancestry is unsubstantiated. Melungeons are generally thought of as American admixtures of Black, White, and Indian cultures referred to in anthropological terms as triracial or triracial isolates. This group is one of the larger and more active communities of contemporary triracial Americans. Melungeons are not quaint asides from early history; they are a lively culture online and off—as book authors, organizers, and educators. They are one of the more fair groups of triracial people, giving pause to the notion of whiteness. The questions raised by Melungeon heritage delight those who are open minded as a blessing, as it gives entree to diverse American cultures. Mixed heritage of these Appalachian people is a notion loathed by others, especially those who have adopted the White European family myth as fact.

Many Americans presumably of European ancestry suspect that they have ties to the Romany, Middle Easterners, or African-descended people.

This idea arises from interpretation of family stories, physical features, inclinations, heirlooms, or photographs.

With the renaissance of Melungeon culture, old theories of their origins are revisited. One such theory asserted by Dr. Swan Burnett in *American Anthropologist* (1889) is that they are part Roma, commonly referred to as Gypsy. Henry Burke an African American anthropologist recently reconsidered the Gypsy as a contributor to Melungeon ancestry. Another scholar, Myra Vanderpool Gormley, investigates the relationship of the so-called Black Dutch to the Melungeon in the paper "In Search of the Black Dutch." *Black Dutch* is a term used by German Gypsies to describe themselves, as is the term *Chicanere.* These people were absorbed into the Pennsylvania Dutch culture after being persecuted in Philadelphia during initial immigrations.

Eminent historian Henry W. Shoemaker, whose work came to prominence in the early twentieth century, is considered an authority on Black Dutch culture. Shoemaker describes the Black Dutch, or Dark Pennsylvania Mountain people, as being of Near Eastern or Aboriginal stock. In a lecture from 1924 he stated that "at least until the 1850s, the men were of medium size, very slim and erect, with good features and large dark eyes. They wore their hair long; very little hair grew on their faces, but they tried to cultivate small side-burns."[24] In a March 31, 1930, *Altoona Tribune* article, he described

> diverse Shekener girls and women . . . of astounding loveliness and their kinship to the so-called Pennsylvania German people, where strange, dark types predominate, was apparent. In fact the Pennsylvania German is but a more cosmopolitan scion of the She-kener . . . and all spring from the same Central and near Eastern polyglot that swarmed into Pennsylvania in the Eighteenth century of diverse origins . . . The Chicenere ranks decimated whenever a chance to settle down came in view; by these judicious marriages, their blood is in the veins of almost every Pennsylvania Dutchman. And the Pennsylvania Dutch boys and girls with their glorious dark eyes, wax-like complexions, wavy dark hair and features of Araby, show the undying presence of forgotten Romany (Gypsy) forbears.[25]

Shoemaker reports on the results of intermarriage between the Pennsylvania Dutch and people of Romany heritage "giving an added dark strain to the already swarthy Pennsylvania German type, fused as it has been from South German, Huguenot, Esopus Spaniard, Hebrew, Swiss, Waldensian, Greek and Indian, the type of the true Pennsylvanian, Tauranian."[26]

For those who are beginning to trace Black Dutch ancestry, a list of characteristics of Melungeons has been established, which includes the following:

- An Anatolian bump, a donut-shaped protuberance on the back of the skull
- Shovel teeth, which are curved across the back rather than straight and end in a ridge at the gum line (commonly found in Native Americans as well)

- History of Familial Mediterranean Fever, an inherited rheumatic disease ethnically restricted to non-Ashkenzi Jews, Armenians, Arabs, and Turks
- Ritualized cleanliness regulations[27]

Common surnames of the Black Dutch include Smith, Mullinses, Mullens, Mullen, Schwartz, Boswell, and Kaiser.

THE RAMAPO MOUNTAIN PEOPLE

Another type of Black Dutch are the triracial people called the Ramapough Mountain Indians, also known as Ramapo Mountain or Ramapough Lenape Indian Nation. Approximately 5,000 of these people are living around the Ramapo Mountains of northern New Jersey and southern New York. The people live northwest of Manhattan, where the New York and Jew Jersey border crosses the Ramapo Mountains.[28] They maintain tribal identity and have a tribal office on Stag Hill Road of Mahway, New Jersey, and since January 2007, their Chief has been Chief Dwaine Perry of the Ramapough Lenape Indian Nation. Legend connects them to the phrase "Jackson Whites," meaning "Jacks," as in Black freedmen, and "Whites," of Dutch, German Hessian, and other Caucasian ethnicities. This name has been rejected by the group as pejorative.

Instead, they are the self-described descendants of the Lenape and Munsee peoples with the admixture of African, Tuscorora, Dutch, and other White ancestry. They claim relationships to other north and western Indian tribes. Their ancestral language is from the Munsee language group, though they speak a patois called Jersey Dutch and mainly speak English.[29]

According to the New Jersey Department of State, there are three groups:

Unalichtigo of southernmost Delaware and Maryland
Unami—southern half of New Jersey
Northern Branch—Minsi-Minisink, "Stony Land" people also called the Munsee

Bands of Munsee include:

Hackensackee
Tappan
Esopus
Canarsie
Wappinger
Ramopough[30]

Historically, between 1630 and 1710, deeds obtained from the Native peoples took away all land between Sandy Hook and Bear Mountain.

Some of the groups moved to the Ramapo Mountains in isolation to try to hold on to land. There were no roads or trails except those started by animals. The land was hard to farm as it was very rocky so the people hunted, fished, and gathered food, growing what crops they could.[31]

THE VAN SALEE'S

Anthony and Abraham Van Salee were the ancestors of the Vanderbilt's, the Whitney's, Jacqueline Kennedy Onassis, and Humphrey Bogart. The Van Salees were among the earliest arrivals to New Amsterdam in the seventeenth century listed as mulatto, son of a Dutch seafarer by the name of Jan Jensen who turned "Turk" and became an admiral in the Moroccan navy. The Port of Salee had been their base. The mother of the two sons was purportedly a concubine from the Middle East. Later ,Anthony Van Salee was asked to leave Manhattan, according to legend because of his uncouth White wife. He was the first settler of Brooklyn—Anthony van Salee—a newer convert to Islam. Van Salee history includes a more contemporary Black branch—Abraham fathered a son with an unknown Black woman. The son became progenitor of his side of the family, which includes Dr. John van Salee De Grasse, born in 1825, who was the first of his race to become an educated doctor. Medical Society of Massachusetts member, Serena, his sister, married George Downing, a successful restaurateur. Abraham used his wealth and power with East Coast's most powerful White families to effect social change. Asked of the connection between themselves and these early-American Black Dutch mulatto's, Mrs. Kennedy insisted the Van Salee's were Jewish. Humphrey Bogart is a Van Salee descendant, and actress Ruth Gordon is a Pendarvis (related family) descendant.

SURNAMES AND APPEARANCE

Surnames often are a way of digging up of family connections such as Onassis-Kennedy's, Gordon's, and Bogart's. Our names are a precious link to the past and can be an unwavering tool when sorting out ethnic connections. Historic surnames of the Ramapo are Van Salee, de Groot, de fries, van der Donck, and Mann.

The Ramapo people and their settlements predate the Revolutionary War—called Tory sympathizers, they have endured suspicion, mistrust, and racism from other groups around them. They have also taken in outsiders with trouble in society such as the freedmen and run-away slaves as well as White and Black women, purportedly of ill repute. The intermarriage has led to features found in other groups that chose to or are forced to live in isolation:

- Syndactyly—fusion of fingers or toes
- Polydactyly—extra fingers or toes

- Pie baldness
- Albinism
- Mental retardation

Described historically as generally a very handsome people with skin complexion ranging from fair to golden bronze, eye color from blue to brown, hair ranging from jet black to entirely white. The outstanding features suggest multiple admixture of Native American, African American, and European Americans from Holland and German extractions.[32]

THE TURKS AND THE MOORS

According to journalists, Khalid Duran and Daniel Pipes in *Faces of American Islam,* Muslim immigrants came to North America as early as 1501, as slaves from Africa. How many Muslim slaves came is up to debate, but scholar, Allan D. Austin, estimates their were about 40,000 brought to what is now the United States. Sylviane Diouf, another expert in this area, puts the numbers higher, estimating between 2.25 million and 3 million in North and South America. While the Muslims from diverse countries were liked by the slave owners, they did not support Islamic beliefs. By the 1860s, importation of Muslim slaves ended.

The slaves that were brought over were concentrated along the southeastern United States, particularly North Carolina—a fate they shared with slaves from Africa. The Melungeons of Appalachia and the Cumberland Plateau who live in remote areas from Virginia to Kentucky may have Muslim (Middle Eastern) ancestry.

Two groups of triracial peoples, the "Moors" and the "Turks of Sumter County" (South Carolina) are believed to be related to Middle Eastern Islamic slaves. In fact, although the American South is thought of in terms of "White" and "Black," South Carolina, in particular, was a multiethnic, multicultural society, all the way back to the colonial era.

The "Free Moors" are believed to be the descendants of Muslims sold into slavery in the Middle East. The Turks of Sumter County are reputedly the descendants of pirates, or escapees from pirates, according to General Sumter who settled in the area. These families also are often reluctant to discuss what they know of their heritage, fearing the stigma attached to Islamic background in the Bible Belt or an association with slavery and pirates. Nevertheless, the groups remain cohesive and an essential part of the fabric of the Carolinian culture.

Just as with the Perkins family previously described, racial tensions that arose prior to the Civil War brought suffering and humiliation to the Melungeon people, the Turks and the Moors. Today, all of these groups are coming out of the dusty annals of American history, demonstrating the vitality and unique contributions of their cultures.

A new multiracial identity reflects a fundamental, postmodern shift in consciousness premised on the "Law of the Included Middle," according to G. Reginald Daniel in his essay, "A New United States Racial Commonsense: Beyond the 1-Drop Rule." To paraphrase, Daniel goes on to state: The included middle seeks to incorporate concepts of "partly mostly" or "both/neither," and acknowledges shades of gray. Although embodied in individuals, the new multi-racial identity is perhaps best views as a montage of new possibilities in the nation's collection racial consciousness whose job is transforming traditional categories and boundaries by expanding definitions of blackness and whiteness.[33]

These first three chapters have been designed to give a historical and philosophical background on the issues of mixed race as it has existed in America from our earliest days. We have examined some of the ethnic and cultural contributions made by the Spaniards, Portuguese, Dutch, Africans, Native Americans, and the English. The next three chapters will visit specific American subgroups that populate the tan territory in between—the place where the nation of mixed-race is the rule rather than the exception or space of an imagined "other."

NOTES

1. Martin R. Delaney, *Principia of Ethnology: The Origins of Races and Color with an Archaeological Compendium of Ethiopian and Egyptian Civilization from Years of Careful Examination and Enquiry* (Philadelphia: Harper and Brothers, 1879), 91–93.
2. Cedric Dover, *Half-Caste* (London: Secker and Warburg, 1937), 203–211.
3. Maria P. P. Root, *Racially Mixed People of America* (Thousand Oaks, CA: Sage Publications, 1992), 3–11.
4. Ibid.
5. Ibid.
6. Itaberi Njeri, *The Last Plantation. Color, Conflict and Identity: Reflections of a New World Black* (New York: Houghton Mifflin, 1997), 216–221, 226–229, 234–236.
7. Ibid.
8. Ibid.
9. Orders Bound by the Mecklenburg County court,1731–36, 133, in Paul Heinegg, *Free African Americans of North Carolina, Virginia and South Carolina from the Colonial Period to about 1820* (Baltimore: Clearfield Co., 2007).
10. Philbeck, Bladen County Land Entries, no. 1210, in Paul Heinegg, *Free African Americans of North Carolina, Virginia and South Carolina from the Colonial Period to about 1820.*
11. Perkins File, T.A.R. Nelson Papers. Calvin M. McClung Collection, East Tennessee Historical Center, Knoxville.
12. Ibid., deposition of Nancy Lipps, 1858.
13. Ibid., deposition of John Nave, 88 years old, 1858.
14. Ibid., deposition of Abner Duncan, 86 years old, 1858.
15. Ibid., deposition of Thomas Cook, 75 years old, 1858.
16. Ibid., deposition of Catherine Roller, 80 years old, 1858.
17. Ibid., deposition of John J. Wilson, about 70 years old, 1858.

18. Ibid., deposition of Anna Graves, 77 years old, 1858.
19. Ibid., deposition of Elizabeth Cook, about 71, 1858.
20. Ibid., deposition of David R. Kinnick, aged 77, 1858.
21. Ibid., deposition of Mary Wilson, 1858.
22. Paul Heinegg, "Deposition of Daniel Stout." *Free African Americans of North Carolina, Virginia and South Carolina from the Colonial Period to about 1820* (Baltimore: Clearfield Co., 2007).
23. Linda Griggs, "Wayfaring Stranger: The Black Dutch, German Gypsies or Chicanere and Their Relation to the Melungeon," April 2000 p. 1, http://sciway3.net/clark/freemoors/Patrin1.htm (accessed October 27, 2008).
24. Henry W. Shoemaker, "1300 Words" cPA Minutes (as of c1900), 1930.
25. Griggs, "Wayfaring Stranger."
26. Shoemaker, "1300 Words."
27. Griggs, "Wayfaring Stranger."
28. David Cohen, *The Ramapo Mountain People* (Saugerties, NY: Hope Farm Books, 1986).
29. Bear Systems, Woodstock, New York, 1995–2008, "The Ramapo Mountain Indians," http://bearsystems.com/JacksonWhites/JacksonWhites.htm (accessed November 10, 2008).
30. Department of State of New Jersey, "Ramapough Mountain," http://www.state.nj.us/state/diversity/american_indian/ramapough.htm (accessed July 9, 2008).
31. Ibid.
32. The Jackson Whites, http://www.bearsystems.com/Jacksonwhites/Jacksonwhites.htm (accessed July 10, 2008).
33. G. Reginald Daniel, *Beyond Black and White: A New United States Racial Order* (Philadelphia, PA: Temple University Press, 2002), 172–175, 189.

CHAPTER 4

Some of America's Best-Known Triracial Groups

AUNT Z'S CHANTING TO THE GUINEAS

I can remember when I visited a certain aunt, living in a New Jersey suburb but born and raised in Richmond, Virginia, who called this person or that a Guinea. She did it with a sting, a pointed-word tool hurled like a burning spear. I'd scarcely heard the term elsewhere and had no idea what it meant, apart from it sounding pejorative, even to young ears.

As an adult, I found a plethora of odd-sounding, sometimes colorful, though still degrading, yet infinitely intriguing names for people. Perhaps in my aunt's case, growing up in Virginia she knew the legend of West Virginia's Guineas people. Perhaps she was using this name, as some people do there, as a slur against Italians. With her having passed on, I'll never really know. I do know that growing up hearing her calling out strange names, finding more groups of people living near us called the Ramapo Mountain People, the Goulds (towners), and Moors, and so many other tiny groups with gigantic ethos about them, I was destined to do this study.

This chapter introduces groups of mysterious people, given even more puzzling names that are woven into the fabric of American folkloric and cultural history. In just about every holler and neck of the woods, you will find singular American groups with a particular connection to place, united through a select list of surnames and sometimes traits, food ways, music, speech patterns and colloquialisms, lifestyle, and spirituality and faith. These historically defined communities may seem islands unto themselves, but they have always interrelated with other groups around them. These are the mixed-race people of the United States who stand strong and apart from the Black, White, red, or yellow categories making their own tan family centered communities. These are the tan people; mixed people with the curious names and colorful stories that populate American history.

THE RED BONES

For example, there are the Red Bones who hold annual conferences in Louisiana. In 2008, the conference's most memorable moment according to their Web site author, Frank Sweet, is very telling:

> The most memorable moment of revelation came when Art Professor, Stacey Webb showed the map of America's triracial communities. By that point in the conference, it had become clear to everyone that there is really only one large triracial community in the southern United States [perhaps wider scaled]. The families of this community migrated freely among regions, seeking only to be left in peace. The many different labels: Redbone, Dominicker, Brass Ankle, Melungeon, etc., are just different derogatory terms given by local people for the same widespread group of people. The map revealed that the different local names simply align along the borders of states. Everywhere that the people migrated, triracial families clustered along boundaries so that they could easily slip back and forth across the border to avoid racial persecution.[1]

This map is indeed a precious finding aiding in understanding the growth and distribution of triracial American communities of families. These groups that have fought hard to encapsulate their fierce sense of pride and singular identity. They have a rich, varied, and colorful patchwork-quilted history in the United States. Still, it is often thought that groups such as the Red Bones and Melungeons began ancestrally as White people who then mixed with Native Americans and African Americans. Some groups started immediately from the union of an interracial couple and continue the strain by intermixing racially to this day.

This book has already begun to deconstruct and expand the meaning of what it is to be African American, showing how it is not a mono-race. The same, as you shall see later in the book, holds true for Native American people. Whites have generally liked being left to being White, shrouded in an impenetrable snowy blanket of whiteness, if you will. Yet the following history of some of America's early settlers and colonizers of the Gulf Coast paints a much different picture.

U.S. TRIRACIAL COMMUNITIES

The Many Shades of Whiteness: The Multiethnic Moors

People of African descent greatly altered the fabric of demographic life in North America. Enslavement developed in the Iberian Peninsula from the eighth to fifteenth centuries; during these 700 years, Islamic Moors from North Africa occupied the peninsula and dominated the populations of Portugal and Spain until 1250 and 1492, respectively.[2]

Islamic inhabitants, who were called Moors, were all complexions. *Moor* could have been used to describe non-Christian Africans of varying skin tones. Most slaves of the fifteenth century were Europeans and North Africans. Palmer, Forbes, and others suggest slavery existed throughout Christendom, practiced by Muslims, Slavs, Egyptians, and Asians also called "Turks," as well as Africans—all potential slaves.

The increase in number of dark-skinned enslaved men and women occurred on the Iberian Peninsula during the fifteenth century. Within this time period, more Berber and black Senegalese slaves arrived (after 1440).[3]

As the Spanish traveled to the New World and attempted to establish southern plantations, Spanish slavery significantly altered, stripping the slave of many pre-established medieval peninsular protections they had come to rely on, including legitimate avenues for *manumission* (obtaining freedom from slavery).[4]

The Racial Triangle

To complicate things further, as far back as the 1600s people of African origin were marrying into the Indian community. Virginia Demarce points out that the east coast "Gingaskins" were intermarrying into both the Black and White communities in large numbers. Both Whites and Blacks are known to have married the Nottoway according to the census of 1808, taken by tribal leaders.

There may be as many as 200 unique family groups with triracial ethnicity, and specific surnames, as well as tight geographic distribution ranges in the United States. Among some of the larger, more well-known groups that have arisen among the triracial communities, many come from clearly defined geographical locations, often within particular counties near specific rivers, mountain ranges, lakes, or other natural features:

1. *Brass Ankles, Red Legs, Marlboro, Turks, Blues* of South Carolina, seem to be descendants of Black Indian admixtures but now show primarily Irish descent and phenotype.
2. *Chestnut Hill People, also called People of the Ridge, Cecil Indians, Guineas, Guinea Niggers, West Hill Indians,* of Maryland and West Virginia especially Philippi Barbour County, north Central West Virginia; related to the Melungeons.
3. *Dominickers*—small multiethnic and multiracial family groups once centered solely in the Florida Panhandle county of Holmes in southern part of the county west of Choctawhatchee River near town of Ponce de Leon. Dominickers are descendants of an interracial couple.
4. *Gouldtowners*—triracial people related to the Lenappe and Delaware live in their own town and surrounding environs in Southern New Jersey and

parts of Delaware. Gouldtowners are also descendants of a "founder" interracial couple

5. *Haliwas* (Haliwa-Saponi) of Halifax and Warren counties in North Carolina. Seventy percent reside within a six-mile radius of town of Hollister in Halifax and Warren Counties, recognized North Carolina state tribe.
6. *Issues* of Amherst and Rockingham County, Virginia.
7. *Ramapo Mountain People (Jackson Whites)* of the New York and New Jersey border
8. *Lumbees, formerly called Croatans,* of Robeson County, Virginia North Carolina, and Upper South Carolina –this is the ninth largest native tribe in the United States.
9. *Melungeons* of Tennessee, and Kentucky (Southern Appalachia) Cumberland Gap area of central Appalachia: east Tennessee, south west Virginia, East Kentucky. A very active engaged community of triracial people though majority Caucasian ancestry from Southern Europe, for example Portugal and near east (Turkey) as well as small traces of Native American and African descent.
10. *Red Bones* of South Carolina and Louisiana (same as above; related to the Melungeons)
11. *We Sorts* is a name for families of mixed-race origins who currently claim descent from the Piscataway native Americans of Charles City Maryland.
12. Members of some of the larger established Indian tribes married into the African and White races, but these groups such as the *Catawbas* are not considered to be triracial but are Native American tribes.

Following are profiles on some of these mixed-race family groups, some of which have loose associations and affiliations with one another.

Brass Ankles

Brass Ankles of South Carolina are a well-known large group of triracial people. Thought to have developed from the offspring of enslaved Indians and Africans—as each group was held in slavery around the same time, with an additional infusion of ancestry from Irish servants from southern plantations. No one is sure where the derogatory name "Brass Ankles" is derived, but there are theories. One is that the people were either runaway slaves or servants who wore brace irons around their ankles when they ran away from enslavement. Another is a commentary on the skin complexion of these mixed-race people who are said to have worn cut-off dungarees that showed their brass-colored ankles (sun-burnt); others believe they were involved with metalsmithing and wore a specific type of handmade brass anklets as a sign of cultural pride. Brass ankles are believed to have small amounts of Indian and African ancestry and to be primarily of Irish descent.

Cajans

The term *Cajan* may throw some people who would take it for an alternative spelling to *Cajun* (Louisiana). However, the Cajan group of people was founded when a Jamaican man married a biracial (Black/White) woman, so it is another case of an entire group formed from a single interracial union. The Cajans married in with the Red Bones and "colored" Creoles expanding their numbers and genetic pool.

Cane River Negroes (The Forgotten People)

The Cane River Creole community consists of descendants of the French, Spanish, Africans, and indigenous people of Caribbean and Americas, other similar mixed Creole migrants from New Orleans, and various other ethnic groups. The region is centered around Isle Brevelle in lower Natchitoches Parish, Louisiana. There are numerous Creole communities within Natchitoches Parish, including Natchitoches, Cloutierville, Derry, and Natchez. Many plantations, some of which were originally run by *Les Gens de Couleur Libre* (freemen of color) are still existent. Isle Brevelle is the area of land between Cane River and Bayou Brevelle. It encompasses approximately 18,000 acres of land, most of which is still owned by the descendants of the original Creole owners. The Cane River Creole family surnames are mostly old French and Spanish in origin. This group enjoyed a hey-day of power, affluence and wealth that far exceeded that of their White neighbors. The original Cane Rive Creoles were often French speaking, and some of the bourgeoisie were educated in Frances best schools, colleges, and academies. A strong artisan class developed around this group and they were renowned for shoemaking, tailoring, ironworking, cigar making, and metallurgy.

Now famous for its coffee stands, the first New Orleans outdoor coffee vendor was a free woman of color, Rose Nicaud—women often owned and ran their own grocery stores and market stands. Many high-profile individuals have arisen from this group in the arts, sciences, and especially in music—the uniquely upbeat-styled jazz called zydeco (which in many languages and patois means "to dance") stems from this area as does several branches of original roots jazz. Artists, especially sculptors working in marble, engravers, ironworkers, woodworkers, and so forth, created the famed gates, fences, balcony details, wooden moldings, balustrades, lamps, shutters, brass fillings, and heavy iron cooking ware still en vogue and in plain sight in Louisiana's cities such as New Orleans. There is a distinctive cuisine that includes elements of the Caribbean, Africa, France, Portugal, Italy, and Amerindian flavors—two of the most famous such dishes are jambalaya and gumbo with so-called dirty rice. Creole language (a patois) is still spoken by the people, with elements of French,

African languages, and Spanish combined with Caribbean elements. The people have a lengthy and lasting relationship with the Catholic Church and with France. For a complete profile of the Cane River Creoles, see chapter 5.

Carmel Indians (Car' mul)

Carmel Indians are a group of mixed-race people called Melungeons who live in Highland County in southwestern Ohio. They are descendants and relatives of Melungeons of Kentucky. They migrated from Kentucky to Ohio in the tenth century. Eight of the nine common surnames among these Melungeons of Magoffin County, Kentucky, go back to African Americans of mixed race in Virginia, Free People of Color, before the Revolutionary War. They are also traced to White mothers, who mixed with Native Americans and people of African descent. Their distribution is North Carolina, Kentucky, and parts of Ohio. Only one family name is associated with the Saponis of North Carolina—the others are mixed-race people who are of Indo-European and sub-Saharan African descent.

Chestnut Hill People

The Chestnut Hill People are a triracial group of families residing just north of Philippi Barbour county in north central West Virginia, usually called Mayles or Mayle or Male as other common surnames. *Guineas,* a pejorative term, has been used toward them because they are thought to resemble Italians. Some Guineas groups have identified with the Melungeons. Guineas have also identified as Native American or Native American and Indo-European. Among the earliest settlers of Barbour in 1890, there was an estimated population of 1,000. It is said that the English ancestor named Male is related to 700 mixed-race people directly. Now the total is around 1,500. These families bear fewer than a dozen surnames: Mayle, Norris, Croston, Prichard, Collins, Adams, and Kennedy. They are also called "the people of the ridge" traditionally they have been subjected to severe ostracism by neighboring Whites.

The Dominickers

The Dominickers are a small group of multiracial and multiethnic families once centered in the Florida Panhandle County of Holmes in southern part of county west of Choctawhatchee River near the town of Ponce de Leon. The Federal Writer's Project (FWP) writers identify Dominickers as descendants of the widow of a pre–Civil War plantation owner and one of her slaves who may have been her husband's mulatto half-brother. The phenotype of these families varies greatly sometimes from convincingly

"White" to totally "Black" in the same nuclear group. They are said to be named after the dominicker chicken which is checkered Black and White coloring.

Lumbee

With approximately 54,000 enrolled members as of the early 2000s, The Lumbee are the ninth largest Native American tribe in the United States. They are centered around Robeson County, North Carolina, and the Robeson River, which they honor by calling it "the Lumbee." Most live in Robeson County and the adjacent counties of Cumberland, Hoke, and Scotland, considered by the Lumbee Tribal Council as the tribe's home territory; some also live in Greensboro and elsewhere. Robeson County communities of Pembroke, Prospect, Union Chapel, Fairgrove, and Magnolia are predominately Lumbee. There are several theories to their existence, including the "Lost Colony" theory proposed in 1884 by Robeson County legislator and local historian Hamilton McMillan and later expanded upon by North Carolina historian Stephen B. Weeks. The theory suggests the Lumbee are descendants of Sir Walker Raleigh's Roanoke Island colonist. The colonists left their settlement, according to the theory, sometime after Governor John White had returned to England in 1587, moving south to an island or mainland location called *Croatoan*—the sole word White and his men found carved in a wooden post upon returning to the island in 1590. There the English colonists are meant to have settled among and intermarried with the friendly Croatan Indians, and by 1650 they migrated to the area of present day Robeson County. While this theory gained popular support, especially when it was argued by historian and author Adolph Dial, John R. Swanton, an anthropologist with the Smithsonian Institution, wrote probably origins of the Lumbee as well in 1933.[5] According to Swanton, the tribe descended mainly from Siouan tribes, primarily the Saura (Cheraw) and Keyauwee. This theory has gained backing by other academics. Lumbee families are tight-knit—children often live near their parents. Most marry within the tribe. Seventy percent of Lumbees were married to another member. Faith, church, and love of church as well as gospel music are central to Lumbee culture.[6] Robeson County has over 130 churches mostly of the Methodist and Baptist faiths. Lumbees appear to be triracial, the descendants of Native Americans, Africans, and Caucasians.

LUMBEE TIMELINE

As far back as the 1750s a reference was made to a small group of Lumbees, about 50 families at that time, who were known to have had members who were mixed bloods. Today the Lumbee are a large and vibrant group of over 40,000, still centered in Robeson County, North Carolina. They are the largest triracial group, and they are vigorously fighting legislation and bureaucracy, both mainstream American and Indian, to be considered a 100 percent Indian tribe.

The Lumbee have a venerable history. They cite acculturation and assimilation as contributing factors to lost languages and lost traditions. Here is a brief timeline:

- 14,000 years ago: Indians settled areas of Southeast North Carolina occupied today by the Lumbee.
- 1714: Lost Colony theory first asserted. Sir Walter Raleigh left colonists in what was then Roanoke Virginia to get supplies from England. When he returned, colonists were gone. Only an inscription in a tree remained. It was suggested that the English had gone to Croatan Island and integrated with the Manteo, an indigenous group.
- 1885: Group first called Croatan Indians.
- 1887: Funding was given to Croatan school.
- 1891: Stephen B. Week wrote article in Papers of the American Historical Association with documentation, maps, and historical accounts of the Croatan or Lumbee people, descended from the colonists at Roanoke.
- 1911: Croatan name changed to Indians of Robeson County.
- 1913: Name changed again to Cherokee of Robeson County.
- 1953: Name changed to Lumbee Indians as many lived near Lumbee River.
- 1956: Federal law recognized them as Lumbee.

It should also be noted that the Lumbee integrated with the Tuscarora Nation, a smaller group in the county. There are, in fact, 18 counties and adjoining areas were the Lumbee live. These include Pembroke, Red Banks, Maxton, Moss Neck, Wakulla, and Rennert.

Lumbee Diversity

The Lumbee defy categorization and don't have a specific look, so they cannot be stereotyped. A Lumbee can be as fair as Heather Locklear or appear to be solely of African or Native American descent. Genetically, they are considered the most "Indian" of all triracial American groups. They not only blended with the Tuscarora people but also the Halteras tribe of Algonquin, Cheraw, and other Siouan people, runaway slaves, free people of color (biracials), and renegade or outlaw Whites.

Lumbee Contributions

- There are prominent figures who are Lumbee, including professors, museum curators, administrations, executives, physicians, ministers, and artists.

- Lumbee people founded the first "Indian"-owned bank.
- They also have their own newspaper called *Carolina Indian Voice.*
- Lumbee are very active in the arts.

Meanness as a Cultural Character

A curious characteristic of the Lumbee, which they profess themselves, is that of *meanness. Meanness* refers to their fierce pride in being Indian. Lumbee sensitivity to insult and a readiness to react to it, sometimes violently defending themselves, leads to the connection with the term *meanness* as well. They are a very cohesive unit, unwilling to bow down to stereotype or categorization dispensed by American legislative acts or even the Bureau of Indian Affairs. The Lumbee are known to have very large families, which contributes to their large numbers.

Melungeons

Melungeon is a term applied to one of a number of triracial groups of the southeastern United States mainly of the Cumberland Gap area of central Appalachia: east Tennessee, southwest Virginia, eastern Kentucky. They have a large concentration of southern European ancestry with some near eastern ancestry, especially from Turkey as well as Middle Eastern, Native American, and sub-Saharan Africa. As many as 200 subgroups exist across the United States.

The people are a loosely affiliated collection of extended families of diverse and unknown origins that migrated and intermarried almost exclusively with one another. The group is considered racially mixed, triracial, and primarily Indo-European in appearance. They typically have dark hair and dark eyes, an olive complexion and have been described as resembling the Portuguese of Europe, Turks of Turkey, Native Americans, and light-skinned African Americans.

A common belief about Melungeons is that they are indigenous people of Appalachia, but that has not been proved. Scholars believe they migrated from Virginia and Kentucky. This mixed-race group most likely developed from Atlantic Creoles of the Chesapeake Bar (Berlin, 1998), freed slaves, and indentured servants of European, African, and Native American ancestry, including Caribbean, Central, and South American Indian, seems to have come together in the creation of what we know today as the Melungeon people.[7] The core family surnames have been traced back to Louisa County, Virginia, in the 1700s (Heinegg, DeMarce, and Goins) and are thought to have been started largely by White women who mated with either enslaved or freemen of color and then set their children free. Melungeons are one of the more prominent, active triracial groups, particularly on the Internet, today.

The most prominent surnames are Collins and Gibson, but Bowling, Bunch, Goins, Goodman, Minor, Wise, Mullins, and Mise are also found within the group.

Ramapough Mountain People

The Ramapough Mountain Indians,[8] also called the Ramapo Mountain Indians or the Ramapough Lenape Nation, are a group of approximately 5,000 people that live around the Ramapo Mountains of northern New Jersey and southern New York. Up until the 1970s, the tribe was referred to as the Jackson Whites, which according to legend is shorthand for Jacks (Blacks) and Whites who have mixed. Many believe they are descendants of runaway and freed slaves called *Jacks* previously and *Whites* of Dutch and Hessian extraction who supported the English during the American Revolution and were forced to escape to the mountains after the end of the war. Most historians believe these to be folkloric tales and mythology not a true history of the group. The members self-identify as Lenape and Munsee descendants with some degree of African, Tuscarora, Dutch, and other Caucasian ancestry. The people claim shared ancestry with other Native American tribes in the north and west. The Ramapough claim their ancestral language was Munsee, but the community has spoken English, as well as Jersey Dutch, a patois in the past.

WE SORTS

"We Sorts" is a name for families of mixed-race origins who currently claim to be descended from the Piscataway Native Americans of Charles City Maryland. They are also called "We Sorts of Mulattos" and "We Sorts of Indians."

Some specific surname patterns appear in the triracial communities. DeMarce cautions the researcher not to hastily conclude that just because the name is the same as yours that a relationship exists. Yet on the other hand, she acknowledges that a specific pattern of name dispersal in a limited population may truly indicate which groups are affiliated with others, indicating a connection to the triracial communities, providing a valuable clue for those searching for such connection.

WHAT'S IN A NAME

"There are niggers who are as white as I am, but the taint of blood is there and we always exclude it." "How do you know it is there?" asked Dr. Gresham. "Oh, there are tricks of blood which always betray them. My eyes are more practiced than yours. I can always tell them."

—Excerpt from *Iola Leroy or Shadows Lifted* by Frances E. W. Harper

Apart from geography, surnames are one of the most important indicators of specific types of triracial identity thus they are shared herein. Some of the naming patterns within each group are as follows:

Brass Ankles: Shavers, Chavers, Chavis
Cajan/Alabama Creole: Chastang
Lumbee: Locklear, Oxendine
Melungeon/Florida Dead Lake People: Mullins, Goins, Collins, Sexton, Gipson, Gibson, Hatfield
Turk: Oxendine, Benenhaley

Heather Locklear

Now, I'm sure that those of you who watch television will be familiar with the celebrity Heather Locklear. She seems to be the quintessential White woman with blond hair (perhaps from a bottle) and light-colored eyes. A more complex picture arises as the result of her name, Locklear.

Locklear is a Tuscarora name that means "hold fast." Locklear's father's side of the family descends from the triracial group called Lumbee. This may not be as clear as the nose on her face but is proved by her traditional Tuscarora name and her family's geographic origins, the land from which the Lumbee hail.

Surnames and Research

Surnames aside, you may wonder why the groups are sometimes called triracial isolates. Generally, it is thought that the name arose from the fact that the groups intermarried, isolating their ancestry from that of others. Indeed, having grown up among several of these groups in southern New Jersey, I observed firsthand the fact that while they might socialize with people who identified with other racial groups, marriage outside the group was strongly discouraged.

Geography also plays a role. Many of the groups were established in remote regions of the country with difficult mountainous terrains. Some areas as noted by the chart above where the groups settled include mountainous areas, lowlands, and swamps as well as rural areas well away from industrialized cities.

FROM SURNAME COLLECTION TO EXTERMINATION: THE DARK ART OF THE EUGENICISTS

While generally surnames are used for genealogical research by individuals wanting to know more about their family history, there is a dark part of our history wherein surnames where collected, archived, and categorized by particular individuals working within the state governments to keep track of people of color who may have been passing for White. Moreover, these records were used in an extermination scheme, a primitive predecessor to the Nazi-style exterminations of World War II Germany, wherein people of supposed "feeble minds" were gathered from the hills and hollers, notably in southern Appalachia but also California, New Jersey, Indiana, and New York, and sterilized or castrated.[9]

TOWARD A "SUPERIOR" RACE: THE DEVELOPMENT OF EUGENICS

Virginia is one of the states where these schemes were particularly well-documented, among some 60,000 people who were forcibly sterilized all across the United States, with almost half taking place in California. In the 1920s until the late 1970s the simple Virginia people who thought they were isolated victims, plucked from their remote mountain abodes or urban neighborhoods, were a part of a larger, decades-long scheme, an American movement of social and biological cleansing determined to obliterate individuals and families deemed inferior.[10]

The intention was to create a new and superior human race. The movement was called eugenics. Conceived at the onset of the twentieth century and implemented by America's most elite, powerful, and learned men and women against the nations most fragile, dispossessed, and vulnerable populations. Eugenicists such as Walter Ashby Plecker and Margaret Sanger sought to methodically terminate all the racial and ethnic groups, and social classes they disliked or feared. In what amounted to nothing short of America's legalized campaign to breed a superior race, eugenicists wanted a purely Germanic and Nordic race that would hold biological dominion over all other types.[11] By using the power of affluence, prestige, and international interchange, American eugenicists exported their burgeoning philosophy throughout the world, not escaping the notice of Germany. Decades after a eugenics campaign of mass sterilization and involuntary incarceration of "defectives" was institutionalized in the United States, the American effort to create a superior Nordic race came to the attention of Adolf Hitler—the rest is history.[12]

Those declared unfit by Virginia did not know it but they were connected to a global effort of money, manipulation, and pseudoscience that ranged from rural America right into the sterilization wards and euthanasia vans of concentration camps of the Third Reich. It comes as no surprise that America had such influence. Within the mainly rural turn-of-the-century populations in places like Indiana and Virginia, existed a small but dedicated epicenter of radical eugenic agitators.[13]

Virginia was eager to take action due to its registrar of vital statistics, Walter A. Plecker, a fervent raceologist and eugenicist. He detested the notion of racial and social mixing in any form. His obsession with White purity turned him into America's preeminent demographic hunter of Blacks, American Indians, and other people of color. Plecker fortified Virginia as the nation's bastion of eugenic racial salvation. His fanaticism propelled him into a lifelong crusade to codify the existence of just two races: White, and every body else.[14] Not simply a southern phenomena, Indiana's house approved the eugenic proposal as well—about two weeks later, with virtually no debate.

In 1907 most Americans were unaware that sterilization had become legal in Indiana. Nor did they comprehend that a group of biological activists were trying to replicate the legislation across the United States. California became the third state to adopt forced sterilization and castration in 1907. New Jersey legislation passed in 1911, followed by New York in 1912. While Virginians of mixed race, or suspected mixed race, as well as those deemed mentally and physically challenged were met with brutality by the eugenicists, so too were Puerto Ricans, especially women, living in major cities, and Native Americans on and off the reservations.[15]

A PURE WHITE RACE?

> In Virginia, you were either ancestrally White, or you weren't.
>
> —Walter A. Plecker

Plecker's passion was keeping the White race pure from any possible mixture with Black Americans, Native Americans, or those of Asian ancestry. The only real goal of his bureaucratic registration was to prevent interracial marriages and social mixing, to biologically barricade the White race of Virginia. As an American Eugenics Society leader, Plecker wrote, "we are attempting to list off the mixed breeds who are endeavoring to pass into the White race."[16] Plecker went on to deliver America's first statewide eugenic registry.[17] The rigid system of registration, which worked toward the Racial Integrity Act, was designed to halt the race mixing and what was thought of as "mongrelization" arising from centuries of procreation by Whites and the enslaved negro as well as their descendants.

According to Plecker,

> when amalgamation between races occurred, one race will absorb the other. And history shows that the more highly developed strain always is the one to go. America is headed toward mongrelism, only . . . measures to retain racial integrity can stop the country from becoming a negroid population. Thousands of men and women who pass for White persons in this state have in their veins negro blood . . . it will sound the death knell to the White man. Once a drop of inferior blood gets in the veins he descends lower and lower in the mongrels scale.[18]

MARGARET SANGER: BIRTH CONTROL AS SOCIAL CONSTRAINT

Margaret Sanger was a zealous, self-confessed eugenicist and she would turn her otherwise noble birth control organization (a predecessor of Planned Parenthood) into a weapon of the eugenicists, who advocated mass sterilization of the so-called defectives. She also argued for mass incarceration of the unfit and Draconian immigration policies. Sanger opposed charitable efforts to uplift the needy and deprived. She argued extensively that it was best to allow them to die off to be replaced by the fit. Sanger saw birth control as the highest form of eugenics.[19] She surrounded herself with some of the eugenics movement's most outspoken racists and White supremacists as she proceeded with her "birth control" programs.

PLECKER'S WAR AGAINST NATIVE AMERICANS

While not one to mix with others from outside the White race, Plecker had a particularly strong hatred for Native Americans. He believed that they had intermixed with generations of Whites and some Negroes, which further irked him. To Plecker, Native Americans were all "mongrels." Plecker embarked upon a serious campaign to eradicate the remaining American Indian's from the face of the earth.[20] He embarked on a systematic method to identify the so-called lower-class descendants of American Indians, who had intermixed with Whites and Negroes and to classify them not as Indian or White, but as "mongrel."

His main targets were the Monacan Indians of Amherst County who descend from the Monacan Confederacy, dated back to Pocahontas's days. Others he pursued included groups we will explore shortly: the Rappahannock, Chickahominy, and Pamunkey tribes. These were small close-knit groups of about 200 people that lived mostly in Rockbridge County, Virginia. With over 200 fairly well-known subgroups of mixed-race people alone, and numerous other mixed ethnic and cultural identities across the United States, Plecker remained hell-bent on having Virginia's citizens register as one of two classifications: White or non-White.

The work of Plecker, Sanger, and countless others of America's most elite, highly educated, and powerful individuals against groups such as the Melungeons, Lumbee, Chickahominy, Rappahannock, Pamukey, and Creoles continues to not only exist but to survive in Virginia and elsewhere. As we shall see in the next chapter, when nurtured and left to their own devices, rather than categorized and manipulated through pseudoscience, mixed-raced groups, such as the Forgotten People and *Gens de Couleur Libres,* create their own unique societies. These societies come to be known nationally and internationally because the citizens excel in many areas of the arts and sciences, making important contributions to the wider culture while at the same time maintaining a tight-knit community.

NOTES

1. Redbone Heritage Foundation, http://www.theredboneheritagefounda tion.com (accessed July 31, 2008).

2. Ethnography Program, "African Nation Founders/Africans in Spanish America. NPS Ethnography: African American Heritage and Ethnography," http://www.nps.gov/history/ethnography/aah/aaheritage/SpanishAmA.htm (accessed July 3, 2008).

3. Ibid.

4. Ibid.

5. The Lumbee Indians, http://linux.library.appstate.edu/lumbee/2/STIL007 htm (accessed July 12, 2008).

6. Jack D. Forbes, *Africans and Native Americans The Language of Race and the Evolution of Red-Black Peoples* (Champaign: University of Illinois Press, 1993).

7. The Lumbee Indians, http://linux.library.appstate.edu/lumbee/2/STIL007 htm (accessed July 12, 2008).

8. Discussed at length in the previous chapter; for the sake of comparison they are listed here as well.

9. Edwin Black, *War Against the Weak: Eugenics and America's Campaign to Create a Master Race* (New York: Thunder's Mouth Press, Avalon Publishing Group, 2004).

10. Black, *War Against the Weak,* 7.

11. "The Lynchburg Story," (Film) released 1993, written and directed by Stephen Trombley.

12. Black, *War Against the Weak,* 7.

13. Ibid., 64.

14. Ibid., 161, 162, 167.

15. Ibid.

16. Letter from Walter A. Plecker to Harry H. Laughlin, February 25, 1928, Truman D-4 3:12.

17. Ibid., 167.

18. "Racial Integrity," *Richmond Times Dispatch,* February 18, 1924.

19. Black, *War Against the Weak,* 127–129.

20. Ibid., 176.

CHAPTER 5

Bricolage: Constructed Identities of *Les Gens de Couleur Libre* and Cane River Negroes

Bricolage is French for taking smaller, well-defined parts or units and assembling them to make something new. Functioning much like a patchwork quilt or assemblage, where intricate, though disparate, parts come together to make a new whole. In the cultural sense of *bricolage,* we are discussing ways mixed cultures have been created by various families and communities in the United States from French, Spanish, African, and Native American cultures, centering the discussion in Louisiana.

> there is no such word as Negro permissible in speaking of this State. The history of the State is filled with attempts to define, sometimes at the point of the sword, oftenest in civil or criminal cases, the meaning of the word Negro. By common consent it came to mean in Louisiana, prior to 1865, slave after the war, those whose complexions were noticeably dark. As Grace King so delightfully puts it, "The pure blooded African was never called colored, but always Negro. *Les gens de couleur,* colored people, were always a class apart, separated and superior to the Negroes, ennobled were it only by a drop of white blood in their veins. The caste seems to have existed from the first introduction of slaves. To the whites, all Africans who were not of pure blood were gens de couleur. Among themselves however, there were covetous and ferociously protected divisions: 'griffes, brisques, mulattoes, quadroons, octoroons,' each term meaning one's degree of transfiguration toward the Caucasian standard of physical perfection. Negro slavery in Louisiana seems to have been early influenced by the Spanish colonies."[1]

ROLE OF THE INTERMEDIARIES

Before we get started, it is important at the outset to understand the backdrop upon which Louisiana, and the rise of the culture of the

Creole, grew. The life of those of African descent on continental North America didn't start in Africa or in the Americas but in an in-between world—a netherworld between the two continents. Always skirting on the periphery of the Atlantic—first in Africa, then in Europe, and finally in the Americas—there was a product of the momentous meetings between these prominent ethnic groups and the indigenous groups of the New World. Although the countenances of these new people of the Atlantic—Atlantic Creoles—might bear resemblance to African, European, and Native American cultures, in whole or part, their beginnings were really apart from either of these locales. Rather, by their experiences and sometimes by their personalities, they had become equal partners in the three worlds that converged in the Atlantic littoral. These groups of people were familiar with the commerce of the Atlantic, fluent in its new languages, and intimate with its trade and cultural practices—they were cosmopolitan, people of the color, in the fullest sense of the words.[2]

Atlantic Creoles traced their beginnings to the historic meeting of European and Africans on the West Coast of Africa during the slave trade. Many of the people of this group served as intermediaries and emissaries, employing their skills with multiple languages and their familiarity with the Atlantic's diverse trade practices, cultural conventions, and diplomatic etiquette, using it to mediate between African merchants, traders, and European sea captains. Some of the Africans were won over by the influence of one party or company or another and entered agreements with particular European trading companies, while Europeans traded with African rulers. Still others operated under their own terms, utilizing their mixed heritage, deploying whichever identity paid off the best. Whatever strategy they adopted, Atlantic Creoles began the process of integrating the icons and beliefs of the Atlantic world into a new lifestyle and unique culture.[3]

ROLE OF THE TANGOSMAOS AND RENEGES

An array of mixed-race people with various tan to deep bronze complexions composed but a small fraction of the population of the coastal factories yet called a disproportionately large amount of attention to themselves. Africans and Europeans alike were revolted by the Atlantic Creoles mixed lineage and all that it suggested. They condemned them as proud snobs that were overbearing in their ambitious desires but realized their necessity to meeting the ends set.

When these Creoles adopted more of the African ways of dress, going so far as wearing traditional power amulets and undergoing circumcision or scarification, Europeans called them *tangosmaos* or *reneges,* meaning "outcasts" in Portuguese.[4]

Conversely, when they took on more European ways of being, wearing European clothing, adorning themselves with religious icons such as crucifixes, giving European names or titles to one another, and generally behaving as White men, Africans denied them the right to hold land, marry, or inherit property. Although the *tangosmaos* faced discrimination, all parties conceded that they were astute traders with a mastery of the finer points of intercultural negotiations perhaps due to their own interracial and intercultural backgrounds. Most found it advantageous to deal with them or through them.[5]

During this period alone, many Creoles rose to positions of wealth and power, compensating for what was viewed as a lack of proper lineage with priceless intercultural knowledge, skills with dealing with diverse populations, and a rare entrepreneurial acumen.

DISPELLING *TANGOSMAOS* MYTHS

- Not all *tangosmaos* were mixed race.
- Not all mixed-race people in the area were *tangosmaos.*
- Despite how our extremely color-conscious society operates today, color was only one indication of this culture and generally the least significant of all identifying factors.

Tangosmaos and the Lingua Franca

Tangosmaos spoke a variety of languages out of necessity including European languages, centered around Portuguese and Spanish, and a Pidgin speech that was called *fala de Guine* or *fala de negros* ("Guinea speech" or "Negro speech") by the Portuguese and Black Portuguese. This language grew in importance to become the lingua franca, for a time, of the Atlantic.[6]

THE CLEMENCY OF DON ANTONIO DE ULLOA

Don Antonio de Ulloa, first Spanish governor of Louisiana was often accused of favoring Creoles of color over Whites. During his brief tenure, as he was expelled in 1766, he repeatedly ruled in favor of the enslaved. The council noted Ulloa had forbidden slaves to be whipped in New Orleans,

QUE SE TENGA POR BLANCO

Under Spanish rule, there was a more open-minded view toward the diverse races of people populating Louisiana. For example, when there was only a sixth of negro blood or Indian ancestry the individual was granted the title *que se tenga por blanco* ("one that considers itself White").

he approved marriages between White men and Black women, and threatened the subjects of France, notably the Acadians, with slavery, "whilst negroes were raised by varying degrees to the dignity of freedmen."[7]

The practice of interracial sexual relationships and marriages in New Orleans accounted for the growth of the class of free people of color. Court testimony concerning mixing between White men and free colored and enslaved women were approved. A few interracial unions were actually sanctioned by the Catholic Church. Some masters assumed full responsibility for the free colored children and legitimized them, thus making them eligible for inheritance. The free colored population increased in numbers, wealth, and influence because of interracial marriages.[8]

CRIOULO, CRIOLLO, AND CREOLE

The Harvard Encyclopedia of American Ethnic Groups defines the word *Creole* as referring to the people, culture, to food and music and to language. Originally from the Portuguese word *crioulo,* the word for a slave brought up in the owner's household, which in turn probably derived from the Latin *creare,* "to create." It became *criollo* in Spanish, *Creole* in French.[9]

Louisianans of French and Spanish descent began referring to themselves as Creoles following the Louisiana Purchase of 1803, to distance themselves from the Anglo-Americans, Black or White, who were then moving into Louisiana from the North and other parts of the South. The word, ever since then has had connotations of "separate," "unequal to," and "other" regarding Black or White people in Louisianan society.

The word *Creole* also has its origins in the Portuguese slave trade. It has been used in Louisiana since the Spanish colonial period to identify native-born Louisianans, descended from the original French speakers of Roman Catholic faith.[10] A Creole was originally a Louisiana-born descendant of colonial ancestors, regardless of whether the ancestors were European, African, or both. Three of the widest used terms were as follows:

- Creoles of color
- White Creoles (Creoles of Indo-European descent only)
- Creole slaves[11]

In the twentieth century, *Creole* referred most often to Creoles of color, ranging in appearance from mixed-race to pure northern Indo-European Whites; Creoles of color brought the Caribbean phenomenon of color to the United States with them. They achieved an elite status for a time in the early nineteenth century; some were slaveholders, and many were landowners. Numerous Creoles of color were educated in the finest schools, conservatories, and academies of France and were patrons of the opera, symphonies, and literary societies. Louisiana's Creoles of color were also noted in the trades and artisan classes for producing finely rendered, much

THE FRENCH-SPEAKING CREOLE CONTRIBUTION

The French-speaking Creoles of Louisiana went to Sainte Barbe Academy and the Couvent School as youths—educated solely in the French language. Some stayed on or went back as adults studying further. Musicians Edmond Dede, Lucien Lambert, and Eugene Victory McCarty all studied composition and other aspects of music at the Conservatory of Music in France. Through this sort of education, mathematician Baside Crocker rose to prominence, as did poet Pierre Dalcour and physicians Oscar Guimbillote and Louis Roddenez. Artist Jules Lion studied lithography and daguerreotype in Paris as well.

sought-after hand-made products. Moreover, they made their mark in the arts, letters, and sciences, as will be explored at the close of this chapter.

GENS DE COULEUR LIBRE AND THE DEVELOPMENT OF THE LOUISIANAN CASTE SYSTEM

The ugly history of slavery in the United States and White ownership of Africans left in Louisiana, as elsewhere in the United States, a traditional association of Whites as superior and upper class, while Blacks comprised the underclass. Mixed people like the Louisiana Creoles saw themselves as separate and apart, as I've mentioned, in some ways dwelling more on their African, Spanish, Caribbean, and mostly their French ancestry than a composite American identity.

Whites entertained feelings of superiority to Negroes and so did Louisiana's *gens de couleur libre.* The degree of privilege or humiliation suffered by a non-White, whether slave or free, was bestowed by society in general based on that individual's placement in the steeped Louisianan caste system.

Upon obtaining freedom, a non-Whites classified as *sacatra* or above entered in a separate but complementary racial category, an intermediate class between White and Black that was seldom recognized outside Louisiana. Under the title of *gens de couleur libre,* free, part-White Creoles were awarded special privileges, opportunities, and citizenship not granted to part-Negroes in other states.[12]

Creoles of color encompassed the majority of free people of color in mid-eighteenth-century New Orleans. This remained true despite migration to Haiti, Mexico, and elsewhere. Free protestant Blacks didn't move to New Orleans en masse until after the Louisiana Purchase. At the time, free Creoles of color were more plentiful, prosperous, and powerful than free Blacks. Apart from members of the artisan class and trades, they were heavily involved in the merchant and bourgeoisie classes, and some were financiers.[13]

CREOLE OF COLOR AND *GENS DE COULEUR LIBRE* ESTABLISHMENTS

Some of the popular vocations for the free colored class were barber, bricklayer, mason, carpenter (was very highly touted), cigar maker, dray-man, rooming-house owner, plasterer, painter, shoemaker, seamstress, tailor, blacksmith, cooper, cook, and butcher.

- Dumas brothers ran an esteemed tailor establishment of Chartres Street.
- Pierre Casenave sold quality retail shoes on Toulouse Street.
- Charles Moore's fine blacksmith shop could be found on Ursulines.
- Charles and Louis Poree sold quality meats at their butcher shop on Felicity.
- Marie Doliol's grocery shop could be found at Urquhart.
- F. C. Boissiere owned the well-respected cigar maker's shop on Marois.

LIFE OF THE IN BETWEENS: LOUISIANA'S "FORGOTTEN PEOPLE"

An example of free people of color, living in between White and Black society, off to and among themselves, are the self-described "Forgotten People." They were described by Private James Holloway in the *Chicago Tribune* as early as 1943 when he made this query:

> "Will someone please give me information about a little place called Cane River Lake Louisiana? . . . The newest towns are Natchitoches and Clouterville. While on maneuvers we had occasion to pass or travel on the bank of this river, or lake, as it is called.
>
> The people there were so nice to us. They gave us coffee and hot biscuits, Creole gumbo, filet and rice. They were a bit shy and they spoke French and broken English . . . Their names are all old French such as DuPre, Chevalier, LeCaure, Mullon, Sarpy, Laubieu, Metoyer, St. Ville, Rachal, Monette and Balthazar. They live in the Old World off to themselves and have their own church, school and places of amusement. When asked who they were, one lady answered in French, 'We are the forgotten people of America' . . . will someone please give me more information before I leave?"[14]

The Forgotten People that had so intrigued Private Holloway were a legendary Creole colony, at home on the Isle Brevelle, area of Louisiana's Cane River country, living there nearly 200 years. Cane River's Forgotten People claim a variety of origins: French, Spanish Indian, and African. Their blend has been cultivated and perpetuated so long that they have been considered, like others groups mentioned in this book, their own distinctive ethnic group, within Louisiana.[15] Neither White or Black, these families of Cane River Colony are simply known as "The People" or "The People of Isle Brevelle." A people with a proud oral history—their legends have been passed down by word of mouth from one family to another.

Cane River's Creoles of color were, despite their unique and separate way of life, a component of a larger social order that was a confraternity, peculiar to Louisiana but existing also in the Caribbean and parts of Africa, from which Blacks were enslaved. *Gens de couleur libre* was a society unto itself where the people successfully rejected identification with an established racial order and achieved recognition as a distinctive ethnic group.[16]

THE STORY OF "COIN COIN" (MARIE THEREZE)

Key to the Forgotten People and Cane River Negroes was an enigmatic former slave, Marie Thereze, also called "Coin coin." Of African descent, she was enslaved in the household of the commandant of Natchitoches Post, Sieur Louis Juchereau de St. Denis. A favored servant, she knew herbal medicine called "rootworking" intimately and dispensed it to save the life of the Madame of the house, Madame de St. Denis. No White or other types of doctors called in from as far as Mexico could cure her elusive disease. Coin coin knew the cure, and Madame de St. Denis's health was restored. In return, the St. Denis family not only manumitted her but also gave her a land grant, with some of the most fertile soil in the colony. Two slaves were given to her, and she purchased more later. Tobacco and indigo were grown.[17]

Coin coin was the first to recognize the rich potential held by the soil to grow indigo, a very important dye plant. In fact, only indigo dye was strong enough to produce the rich blue colors needed for the uniforms of European armies, so Coin coin had a built-in, lucrative business which needed steady supply. Other agricultural and nonagricultural products were also grown at Melrose. For example, she and her slaves hunted bears for their grease, which they also exported to Europe, where it was popular as a lubricant for axles of carriages and artillery pieces.

CANE RIVER LIFESTYLES

Coin coin's plantation was called Yucca Plantation. More commonly known as Melrose, it consisted of constructed buildings in West African–style adapted to Louisiana conditions and local materials. Marie Thereze was a family woman as well as a visionary and entrepreneur. Most of her children were of Franco-American descent resulting from an alliance with a Frenchmen at Natchitoches Post. Claude Thomas Pierre Metoyer, a man from the merchant class bourgeoisie of Ranch, was the father of her children and her companion most of her life.

For 50 years the Metoyers of Cane River enjoyed wealth and prestigious status few Whites of the era matched. Cordial and striking manor homes were erected on every plantation on the river, furnished only with the finest artisan furniture and accoutrements made by local and European artisans.

The colony was founded by the Metoyers, who found ways of skirting the miscegenation laws that were supposed to be upheld by the local priests. At one time Coin coin was even listed as her husband's slave to achieve desired ends.

Each successive generation, however, included the introduction of more family names from the *gens de couleur libre* as well as from Haiti and New Orleans. Those who passed inspection were allowed to intermarry within the community. Even wealthy White planters of the local parishes arranged marriages for their "children of color," to offspring of the Metoyers.

The fresh influxes of genetic lines protected the Forgotten People from the genetic hazards of family intermarriages, which some of the other historic mixed-race groups included in this study have suffered.

Creating their own self-sustained communities, the Forgotten People founded their own schools, churches, businesses, and places for entertainment. Grand Pere Augustin (the clan's patriarch), eldest son of Marie Thereze, served for decades as judge and jury of the community. His vision was to make the isle a refuge offering respite for his people, against a new breed of what he considered greedy Americans.

THE RISE AND FALL

The story of free people of color in Louisiana is a dramatic one of increasing population, accomplishments, and prosperity, and then drastic decline, especially in terms of population growth and wealth.

Stringent laws against Free People of Color (FPC) grew to their height in 1830:

1825—FPC no longer allowed to enter the state.
1830—It became illegal to publish, write, or print anything that might produce discontent with the colored population (life imprisonment or capital offense).
1831—Expulsion reserved for undesirables was vetted against FPC freely.

SOCIAL AND ECONOMIC DOWNTURN

A nationwide economic depression and increasingly restrictive legislation began to curtail the economic activities of the colonies by the mid-1800s. Several plantations, including Yucca (Melrose), were lost.[18]

Despite the losses, the colony itself continued to prosper until the Civil War began. Cane River's *gens de couleur libre* supported the doomed cause of the Confederacy—they suffered from the ravages of the war, including the financial ruin of the Reconstruction. After Reconstruction, unlike White planters, their ruin was complete in a reactionary political climate that

ETYMOLOGY OF *COIN COIN*

Called variously *Choera, Kiokera, Quoinquin,* and *Keun Kwoin,* Marie Thereze's name is believed to derive from the African linguistic group of the Gold Coast, Dahomey region. *Coin coin* is a linguistic clue to her origins—*Ko Kwe* is reserved for second-born daughters in the *Glidzi* dialect of the Ewe people occupying the coastal regions of Togo. Marie Thereze was second born daughter of Francois and Marie Francois. The parents were of African descent, though they possibly had other admixtures of the Caribbean or of Amerindian origin, like the other people of the area. They did cling to their African heritage proudly. At least three of their children were given African names, used in great frequency when referring them in the family.

Coin coin was quite a catch, speaking French, Spanish, and an African dialect as well as being trained as a rootworker (medicine woman). It was not long before Metoyer persuaded Mme. De Soto to lease him her Negro slave. In payment for her services, he promised her owners to provide her with room and board; Marie Thereze moved in with Metoyer. The two bore numerous children between 1769 and 1776. While the Metoyers had to try many different ways of securing their relationship over time, there were many other ways the *gens de couleur libre* made formal and informal arrangements for establishing interracial relationships, skirting laws and convention.

turned against Blacks and *gens de couleur libre* of all castes and shades. Celebration elsewhere of emancipation was hearty, yet for the peculiar people of Isle Brevelle, the Forgotten People as it were, found themselves enslaved and disenfranchised once all other men were set free.[19]

PLACAGE AND THE ARRANGEMENT BALLS

The quadroon balls are places to which these young creatures are taken as soon as they have womanhood, and there they show their accomplishments in dancing and conversation to the white men who alone frequent such places. When one of them attracts the attention of an admirer, and he is desirous of forming a liaison with her, he makes a bargain with the mothers, agrees to pay her a sum of money, perhaps 2000 dollars or some such sum in proportion to her merits as a fund upon which she may retire when the liaison terminates. While in this arrangement she is "une placee" 'one who is placed' or spoken for, somewhat akin to a mistress.[20]

Placage was the practice that existed in Louisiana and other French and Spanish slaveholding territories whereby women of color (the choice of legal marriage denied them) entered long-standing, formalized relationships with White European men. Once an agreement was reached, the girl was spoken of as *une placée*. This gave her a status similar to an honorable marriage and secured her future. Custom dictated that the man buy a small home on or near *rue de Rampart* and present it to her. Until the house was completed, he never saw the young woman without her chaperone.

Taking It a Step Further: Bal de Cordon Bleu

In New Orleans a class of affluent families of color became known as the *cordon blues*. It is their class that gave rise to the famed *Bal de Cordon Bleu*. Thought of as a way to facilitate their survival as a race, the *Bal de Cordon Bleu* was an elegant affair similar to a debutante ball. It was at these balls that the proudest quadroons and other Creoles of color were reduced to representing their daughters to wealthy European men for the purpose of arranging a life partnership. The festive affairs took place under highly controlled environments with as much decorum as possible.

Folk belief holds that the first of these balls originated at the end of the eighteenth century, while Louisiana was controlled by Spain. They are said to have lasted "for nearly a hundred years,"[21] degenerating only after the Civil War, wherein they turned to shabby, ill-mannered affairs with no semblance of the elegance and panache of their hey-day.

Though seldom noted, the *Bal de Cordon Bleu* was very different from the Quadroon Balls of *les gens de couleur libre*. *Bal de Cordon Bleu* presented what were considered the highest quality, upper echelon women who were the most cultured and purportedly stunning. With the racist conventions of the time, this also means they were the most highly mixed, bearing as little resemblance as possible to Africans or Amerindians.

Bal de Cordon Bleu was also called a Society Ball and many other names. It was sponsored by the *Société Cordon Bleu*, an organization of wealthy quadroon matrons who used the balls as a way of securing for their daughters *placage* arrangements with high-born White Creole men. Each mother's purported aim was to procure a so-called protector for her daughter. Some feel the girls were bartered into concubinage and sold as slaves by their own mothers. Mostly it is agreed that the young women were already raised as an elite class of females and were only use to the finest things in life. The mothers then are thought to have been looking out for their daughter's best interest, helping them maintain their lifestyles for as long as possible but this is all debatable depending from which lens you are viewing. The by-invitation-only ball, was seen as a means of ensuring that the young daughters of these well-to-do Creole families would not face life alone. In order to make sure that *placage* worked as it was intended, only wealthy men were invited to attend the *Bal de Cordon Bleu,* stipulated by the hefty price for entry.

TIGNON LAW OF 1786

In Louisiana, regardless of the prescription of the *Bal de Cordon Bleu,* all of the mixed-race women were considered exceedingly beguiling and dazzlingly exotic. In response to the angry outcries of White females, Governor Miro enacted on June 2, 1786, his infamous "*tignon* law," which made excessive attention to dress by women of pure or mixed African blood, a criminal offense. The women were forced to refrain from wearing fine clothes or jewelry they owned, nor could they wear feathers or jewels in their hair, and ultimately, they had to cover their hair with kerchiefs called *tignon.* This was designed to realign the women with their roots in enslavement, humbling them and reminding the men that they were "other," even if some of them looked White or were found to be attractive. However, despite the law, colonial European men still found these women elegant and striking, and in many cases, they were the preferred women of the day.

SURVIVAL INSTINCTS

It is true that there was also the gender imbalance I have spoken of often in these pages. The conditions in the territory essentially guaranteeing long-term sexual arrangements between White men and free Black women were tolerated in part because New Orleans was often ravaged by disease and death due to its semitropical climate and its terrain, which resulted in infamous mosquito infestations. Diseases such as smallpox, influenza, yellow fever, and malaria were common and often decimated the White populations. Children were most vulnerable to diseases, while women tended to die in childbirth.

- The median age of death for White males was 30.6 years, and for White females 18.1 years.
- The figures for free Blacks were far more dismal; for free Black males, it was 8.1 years of age, while for free Black females, it was 30.3 years.

Interracial unions and the offspring they produced resulted, at least in part, from these grim demographic circumstances, as well as from a shortage of White women and abundance of free Blacks and enslaved women. Considering these statistics, those who belittle the free woman of color for her decision to engage the affections and support of a White male choose to ignore the basic demographic facts—she had little choice.[22]

PARAMOURS OF CHOICE

Interracial liaisons were common for many reasons other than demographics. There is evidence that White men chose their mixed-race paramours intentionally and not just because there were fewer White women. The precedent had already been set, outside the United States, in St. Dominique, where French planters took only the finest enslaved women for their mistresses. Many of these women were described as handsome with thick, black wavy hair and straight features. By carefully selecting women in St. Dominique, women of an exotic mixed-race beauty similar to the high-born Hindus of India in look were created.[23]

THE FORGOTTEN PEOPLE OF TODAY

Distribution and Surnames

The Cane River Creole community is still made up of people with French, Spanish, African, and Native American ancestry, other similar Creole migrants from New Orleans, and various other ethnic groups who inhabited the region. It centers around Isle Brevelle in lower Natchitoches Parish, Louisiana. There are many Creole communities within Natchitoches Parish, including Natchitoches, Cloutierville, Derry, and Natchez. Many plantations still exist. Isle Brevelle, the area of land between Cane River and Bayou Brevelle, includes approximately 18,000 acres of land, the majority of which (16,000 acres) is still owned by the descendants of these original Creole families.

The Cane River Creole family surnames, which are of French or Spanish origin include Metoyer, LaCour, Coutee, Monette, Bathazar, Sylvie, Moran, Rachal, Conant, Beaudion, Darville, LaCaze, Pantallion, Mullone, Severin, St. Ville, Llorens, Delphin, Sarphy, Laurent, DeSoto, Christophe, Honore, Chevalier, DeSadier, Anty, Dubreil, Roque, Clouteir, LeVassuer, Meziere, Bellow, Gallien, Conde, Porche, and the Dupre.

Regions of our country and abroad with significant Creole populations include Louisiana; East Texas; Los Angeles County, California; coastal Mississippi; Chicago; coastal Alabama; Veracruz, Mexico; Haiti; Puerto Rico; Cuba; the Dominican Republic; and France.[24]

Language

The language forged by the Black Creoles, which is a fusion of French, Spanish, and West African languages, is still spoken in central Louisiana today. Creole French is still spoken in New Orleans. Whites of French/Spanish mixture were referred to as French Creoles. The mixed-race population was referred to as African Creole, Black Creole, mixed Creole, Creoles of color, and *gens de couleur libre.*

Zydeco: Distinctly Creole Roots Music

Zydeco, which means "*les haricots,*" or "snap beans" in English, is a form of American roots music that evolved in the late 1800s, a development in the African-inspired call-and-response vocals of the Black and mixed-race French-speaking Creoles of south and southwest Louisiana. Typically, it is an up-tempo beat, dominated by the sounds of the button or piano accordion and a form of washboard called "rub-board" or *frottoir*. The Zydeco Rubboard (*Frottoir*) is recognized around the world as a cultural icon of Louisiana. Zydeco music was originally created at house dances were Blacks and *gens de couleur libre* of south Louisiana gathered and socialized. Gradually, the music moved to the Catholic Church community centers and from there to rural dance halls and nightclubs.

Code Noir

The Creoles of color enjoyed many freedoms due to the Code Noir, set of laws established in 1724 by the French—this afforded the right to own land, a privilege lacking elsewhere in the country. Thus, there was more space and freedom to gather and act expressively through music and the arts.

An Intercultural Form

Zydeco music incorporated waltzes popular during the time as well as shuffles, two-steps, blues, and rock and roll. Today the tradition continues to evolve and change, now encompassing brass band, ska, rock, Afro-Caribbean, reggae, hip-hop, R & B, and soul rhythms. Amédé Ardoin made the first recordings of Creole music in 1928. This Creole music served as a foundation for what later became known as *zydeco*—a word that became synonymous in many different languages with the words "to dance."

Zydeco's Movers and Shakers

1. In the mid-1980s, Rockin' Sidney brought international attention to zydeco music with his hit tune "My Toot Toot."
2. Clifton, Rockin' Sidney, and Queen Ida all garnered Grammy awards during this seminal period in the genre, opening the door to the emerging artists who would continue the traditions. Ida is the only living Grammy award winner in the genre.
3. John Delafose was wildly popular regionally, and then the music took a major turn because during this time there were emerging bands coming onto the national scene infusing a vibe of new sounds and styles within the music. Boozoo Chavis, John Delafose, Roy Carrier, Zydeco Force, Nathan and The Zydeco Cha Chas, The Sam Brother, Terrance Simien, and Chubby Carrier helped update the music with unique innovations of their own.
4. Zydeco superstar Buckwheat Zydeco was already well into his career and signed his major label Island Records deal also in the mid-1980s. All of these

things combined with the popularity of Cajun and Creole food nationally, and the feature film *The Big Easy* led to a resurgence of the zydeco music traditions, cultivating new artists while the music took a more innovative direction for increased mainstream popularity.

5. Young zydeco musicians, such as C. J. Chenier, Chubby Carrier, Geno Delafose, Terrance Simien, Nathan Williams, and others, began touring internationally during the 1980s.
6. Beau Jocque was a monumental innovator who infused zydeco with powerful beats and bass lines in the 1990s, adding striking production and elements of funk, hip-hop, and rap.
7. Young performers like Chris Ardoin, Keith Frank, and Zydeco Force added further by tying the sound to the bass drum rhythm to accentuate or syncopate the backbeat even more. This style is sometimes called "double clutching."
8. Now there are hundreds of zydeco bands continuing the music traditions across the United States and in Europe. A prodigious 9-year-old zydeco accordionist, Guyland Leday, was featured in an HBO documentary about how deeply music is felt by young people.
9. Zydeco became its own category in the Grammy awards. The "Best Zydeco or Cajun Music Album" category was created for 2007, and the 2007 nominations went to Le Cowboy Creole by Geno Delafose & French Rockin' Boogie; King Cake by Lisa Haley; Live: Á La Blue Moon by Lost Bayou Ramblers; Blues De Musicien by Pine Leaf Boys; Racines by Racines; the La Louisianne Sessions by Roddie Romero and the Hub City All-Stars; and the winner, *Live! Worldwide by Terrance Simien & The Zydeco Experience.*
10. Today, because of the migration of the French-speaking Blacks and multiracial Creoles, mixing of Cajun and Creole musicians, and the warmth of people from outside cultures, there are widespread hotbeds of zydeco including Louisiana, Texas, Oregon, and California, and even Europe as far North as Scandinavia.

CREOLE ARCHITECTURE

French Creole architecture is an American colonial style that developed in the early 1700s in the Mississippi Valley, especially in Louisiana. French Creole buildings make use of stylistic traditions of France, Spain, Caribbean, and many other origins.

French Creole homes from the colonial period were thoughtfully designed for the hot, wet climate of that region. For natural cooling purposes, traditional French Creole homes had some or all of these features:

- Timber frame with brick or *bousillage* (mud combined with moss and animal hair)
- Wide-hipped roof extends over porches
- Thin wooden columns

- Living quarters raised above ground level
- Wide porches, called "galleries"
- No interior hallways
- Porches that served as passageway between rooms
- French doors (doors with many small panes of glass) that open from the center

As noted, the architecture at Melrose (Yucca Plantation) is modeled off west African rural, rounded buildings with thatched roves. There is also a deep relationship with the architecture of France shared in New Orleans. Notable features of the buildings are the fine iron-working, which was done largely by Black Americans and *gens de couleur libre* during the development of cities such as New Orleans. Moreover, the cemeteries are notable. Out of necessity because of the water tables, the graves are tombs placed above ground. Many Africanisms are also apparent in the grave architecture, including the use of so-called last-touched objects displayed on the grave site the decorations with whitewash, an other-worldly/spirit-world color, and the placement of seashells as adornment on the tombs.

CUISINE

Louisiana Creole cooking is recognized internationally—originating in New Orleans, making use of the holy trinity of ingredients (chopped celery, bell peppers, and minced onions). Cajun cuisine is similar but has a large variety of European, French, Caribbean, and African as well as Amerindian influences. Gumbo is a traditional Creole dish. It was created in New Orleans by the French attempting to make bouillabaisse in the New World. The Spanish contributed onions, peppers, and tomatoes; from Africa comes the okra, fritters, porridge such as grits, yams, watermelon, tamarind, ackee, dates, figs, goat, black-eyed peas, and stewing technique; the American Indians contributed file—ground sassafras leaves as well as other tempting spices; and later, the Italians added garlic. The Germans contributed potato salad as a side dish and started the practice of eating gumbo with a bit of potato salad on it. The stew itself consists of shrimp, crab, sausage and oyster, chicken sausage, gumbo chicken and sausage, spices, and the holy trinity. Other popular Creole foods include bananas Foster, pain perdu, red beans and rice, and jambalaya as well as blackened seafood and poultry.

THE QUINTESSENTIAL MIXED-RACE CULTURE

In the popular American imagination, the Creoles of color of Louisiana are the quintessential embodiment of a vibrant and visible mixed-race culture. In fact, the culture itself is so rich that it has left an indelible mark on American's cuisine, music such as jazz and zydeco, and its colorful language. As a cultural garden, there couldn't be another place better suited to growth than the warm, flexible, humid, accessible open territories of Louisiana. New Orleans *gens de couleur libre* studied and expatriated to France as early as 1740, and emigration culminated in 1840. During the 1800s, France served as a spiritual home for the Creoles of color who were suffering from increasingly strict laws and restrictions in their homeland of Louisiana.

While historically much time is spent recording the downtrodden history of people of color around the world, the next chapter paints a different picture. It demonstrates that high-born people of mixed race were not an Americanism but could be found across Europe, particularly centered in its royal families, beginning with Italy's House of Medici.

NOTES

1. Alice Moore Dunbar-Nelson, *A Reader* (Lanham, MD: University Press of America, 1979).
2. Ira Berlin, *Many Thousands Gone: The First Two Centuries of Slavery in North America* (Cambridge, MA and London, England: The Belknap Press of Harvard University Press, 1998), 17.
3. Ibid.
4. Ibid., 19.
5. Ibid., 20.
6. Ibid.
7. Violet Harrington Bryan, "Marcus Christian's Treatment of Les Gens de Couleur Libre," in *Creoles: The History and Legacy of Louisiana's Free People of Color*, ed. Sybil Kein (Baton Rouge: Louisiana State University Press, 2000), 47.
8. Ibid., 48.
9. *The Harvard Encyclopedia of American Ethnic Groups* (Cambridge, MA: Belknap Press of Harvard University, 1980), 247.
10. Lester Sullivan, "Composers of Color of Nineteenth-Century New Orleans: The History behind the Music," in *Creoles: The History and Legacy of Louisiana's Free People of Color*, ed. Sybil Kein (Baton Rouge: Louisiana State University Press, 2000), 73.
11. Ibid., 73.
12. Ibid., Preface, xiv.
13. Ibid.
14. Gary Mills, *The Forgotten People: Cane River's Creoles of Color* (Baton Rouge: Louisiana State University Press, 1977), xxv.
15. Ibid.
16. Ibid., xiii.
17. Ibid., xxv.
18. Ibid, xxviii.
19. Ibid.
20. "Free Colored Class of Louisiana," 14–7. Christian quotes from Frederic Law Olmsted, *A Journey in the Seaboard Slave States* (New York: Dix and Edwards, 1856); Harriet Martineau, *Society in America* (Paris: A & W Galignani, 1837); and G. W. Featherstonbaugh, *Excursion Through the Slave States* (New York: Harper and Brothers, 1841).

21. Joan M. Martin, "Placage and the Louisiana Gens de Couleur Libre," in *Creole: The History and Legacy of Louisiana's Free People of Color* ed. Sybil Kein (Baton Rouge: Louisiana State University Press, 2000), 65.

22. Kimberly S. Hanger, "Coping in a Complex World: Free Black Women in Colonial New Orleans," in *The Devil's Lane,* ed. Catherine Clinton and Michele Gillespie (New York: Oxford University Press, 1997), 220.

23. Joan M. Martin, "Placage and the Louisiana Gens de Couleur Libre: How Race and Sex Defined the Lifestyles of Free Women of Color," in *Creoles: The History and Legacy of Louisiana's Free People of Color*, ed. Sybil Kein (Baton Rouge: Louisiana State University Press, 2000), 61.

24. Ethnologue Report for Language Code:lou, "Louisiana Creole French," http://www.ethnologue.com/show_language.asp?code=lou (accessed November 14, 2008).

CHAPTER 6

From Italian Explorers to Sicilian Contandini and Biracial Royals: The Mixed-Race Experience as Illustrated by the Italian Diaspora

THE DREAM

999 Afro-Americans arranged in a line—not by height or age—but chromatically, from darkest to lightest, lightest to darkest. Colors blending slowly, imperceptibly into one another. Not just colors, but lips, noses, and types of hair too . . . light people with thick lips and wide noses, dark people with thin noses and straight hair. Enter a White person to take her place in line. Does she go to the end? No, for she isn't the palest one there, not by far. After much searching she finally finds one who looks similar to herself, so much so, they could be sisters. The only difference between them is that the Black woman's eyes are blue, while her own are brown. Meanwhile, the color line has begun to curve in on itself—enveloping her pushing her up against her near-truth—until finally it engulfs itself and dissolves.[1]

—Rainier Spencer

Between 30 and 70 percent of all African Americans, according to multigenerational history, are multiracial. Almost every Latino or Hispanic and Filipino is multiracial, as are the majority of American Indians and indigenous Hawaiians. Less noted but equally true, a significant amount of White-identified people are multiracial. The way the U.S. Census Bureau has recorded data on race made it difficult to ascertain the correct number of biracial or multiracial people in the United States.[2]

Actually whether the Census Bureau records information correctly or inclusively is in a way irrelevant. Over 100,000 Blacks have passed over into White society[3] and not just ordinary society but some of the highest societies we recognize. The jury is already in and has been for years: biological races don't exist now, nor have they ever. Everyone is always already mixed.

According to race study professor, Jayne O. Ifekwunigwe in London:

> We are all African, only some of us have been "away" longer than others. That said, for as long as modern humans have populated the earth and migrated within and across continents, intergroup mating and marriages have been inevitable and commonplace. As such, there are no discrete or pure biological "races." In fact, there is more variation within a group that is socially designated a race than between groups socially designated as different races.[4]

These facts make the story of southern Italians, Italian and European royalty, and the immigrant Italian American all the more compelling and significant to this telling of multiracial history.

RACE CASTE AND MATTERS OF LIFE AND DEATH

In our society, a political, sociological, and psychological desire has been steadily fed—this sci-fi sociological beast constantly demands a dominator and others to be dominated—a class is developed through the beast, which maintains its own caste, assigned by race or geography. Typically, such a group consists of mixed ethnicity or mixed-race people marred by chronic imposed psychological or political disability such as enslavement or limited access to immigration, socio-economic development, or educational opportunities.

Those considered White cling on to the notion of whiteness to maintain their rights and privileges while remaining out of the spotlight that would cast them into the underclass of "others." The life and death situations arising out of legal and societal rights and privileges created the environment for darker-skinned Whites such as Italians with known or suspected mixed heritage to stand in stark juxtaposition to the enslaved "other." Many multicultural Americans, including those of Italian ancestry, point to Blacks as the "not-me" or "other" group of folks, while demanding their true ethnicity is recognized as exoticized but monoracial.[5]

The vocabulary and thought processes connected to mixed-race dialogue necessitates an agreement that there are certain people of color, while others are colorless, monoracial, in other words, White. Occasionally, Whites speak of being mixed; it is usually in a religious connotation (interfaith) or some variation of European ethnicities. Racial mixture and whiteness are psychologically antipathetic because "White" has been designated as a signifier of purity, posing a problem for the southern Europeans with varied phenotypes and a history of intense interrelations with non-White cultures.[6]

We know that generally American society accepts the idea of *mestizaje*, if by no other means than the hoards of legislation generated in the past 370 years, governing the determination of racial identity in our society.

The existence of words such as *mulatto, quadroon,* and *octoroon* provide evidence. We also know because of court cases and because of blood quanta. We are all mixed—not just as visible mulattoes but everyone else as well.[7]

Being multiracial in a hierarchal system such as nobility, whether pluralist or integrationist or both, might suggest the individual is a little less Black and thus a little less subordinate. However, it does not assure equality with Whites. The challenge is completely to dismantle the Eurocentric undermining of the racial order in the United States and elsewhere through the deconstruction of both dichotomous and hierarchical relationship between Blacks and Whites by making a sincere social commitment to affirming the equality of differences in an egalitarian, pluralistic manner while concurrently accepting the equality of commonalties in the manner of egalitarian integration.[8]

Peering into the window of the bastion of high White society, investigating the blood lines of nobility affords an opportunity to deconstruct closely held false notions about the White race being an exclusive, pure-blood society.

A BRIEF HISTORY OF SOUTHERN EUROPE AND THE MULTIRACIAL EXPERIENCE

The Mediterranean slave trade to the ancient world moved sub-Saharan Africans into North Africa and southern Europe, and moved Black Sea Europeans into north and sub-Saharan Africa. The transatlantic slave trade ensured contact between southern and northern Europeans, sub-Saharan West Africans, and the indigenous peoples of North and South America—there you have a rich, turning, boiling—melting pot of cultures united through geography and singular purpose.[9]

> By 1470, 83% of the slaves in Naples slaves were sub-Saharan Africans. There were also African slaves already in Sicily. Their perceived inferiority was entwined in the tapestry of European cultural folklore. Italian and emerging European racism was examined by William Shakespeare in Othello (1604). That racism was a topic of this major work indicates that racist ideas concerning Africans had to have begun to spread to England rapidly. Elizabethan literature abounded with lecherous and degenerate portrayals of black men. These characters were used to fulfill the dramatic expectations of this period, whereby a man's color revealed his villainy.
>
> —*Joseph Graves*[10]

Discoveries and Miscegenation

The era of discoveries led by Europeans seeking New Worlds such as Christopher Columbus presented a massive opportunity for miscegenation. Most often the sailors and ship crew were all male, and they were not monoracial. Christopher Columbus purportedly brought a ship to the Gulf States region of the United States in the early 1500s, years before the Virginia Company's predominately English ships arrived, leaving Italian and formerly enslaved African-Italians to make their way in the Americas, without Italian or African-Italian women. Typically, with these explorative trips it took over a decade before women of the same culture were imported to the new world to form families. This suggests that from our early presence as non-native Americans, there has been a confluence of miscegenation between southern European explorers and their crews, with Native Americans, Africans already enslaved in the Americas, freedmen, other Whites of various origins, and those brought over on the ships with the explorers.

In 1842, it was said that "in the Atlantic States the population is Teutonic and Celtic; whereas, in the Gulf cities, there is a preponderance of the blood of the Italian, Spanish, Portuguese, French, and other dark-skinned races."[11]

The reason is simple to the historian. Our states along the Gulf of Mexico where chiefly colonized by emigrants from southern Europe. Such European colonists belonged to types genealogically distinct from the white-skinned Pilgrim fathers who landed north of Florida.

Thus, Spain when her traditions begin, was populated principally by Iberians. France received a considerable transfusion of the same blood through the Basque provinces. Italians are dark. Such races blended in America with the Negro, generally giving birth to a hardier and therefore more prolific stock than White races such as Anglo-Saxons produce by intercourse with Negresses.[12]

THE MYTH OF *LIMPIEZA DE SANGRE* (PURE BLOOD)

While pure blood, 'limpieza de sangre', was held at a premium, particularly among the noble families of Europe, in a 15th century defense of 'conversos', Bishop Lope de Barrientos lists a veritable Who's Who of Spanish nobility, as having conversos members or being of converse descent and would point out that given the near-universal conversion of Iberian Jews during Visigothic times, who among the Christians of Spain could be certain he is not a descendant of those conversos.

—Norman Roth[13]

CONVERSOS

Conversos is Spanish and Portuguese for a "convert," from the Latin *conversus*, "converted, turned around." The feminine form is *conversa*. It referred to Jews or Muslims or descendants of Jews or Muslims who converted or were compelled to convert to Catholicism in Spain and Portugal during the fourteenth and fifteenth centuries.

Contandini

Most of the Italians who emigrated to the United States were peasants and manual laborers who came from the economically deprived, undereducated, and underdeveloped southern agricultural provinces of Basilicata, Calabria, Campania, Puglia, and Sicily. These southern Italians had a history of colonial subjugation. They were already considered racially "other" by the northern Italians ruling classes.

Enhancing their status of "other" was Italy's history of African, Arab, Greek, Norman, and Spanish settlements, which defied theories of racial purity. This coupled with the Italian southerner's darker complexions and what was perceived by others as "primitive" ways, offered the proof needed by many northerners, to support their discriminatory ideas that these were a separate and racial inferior group of people. Southern Italy is more an imaginary realm spatially than a geographical reality, however. In terms of racist connotations, its scope conveniently excludes Rome, Sardinia, and Abruzzo and instead uses the conceptual space called southern Italy as a synonym for anarchy, rebelliousness, poverty, and lack of culture but only in selected southern areas.

WHERE ARE ALL THE "OTHERS"?

When considering groups of people who fall outside the neat categories of Black, White, red, brown, or yellow, many look toward southern Europe. There we find people who often have dark, thick, curled or waved hair, olive to deep brown skin, dark brown eyes—in other words, characteristics usually attributed to those with multiracial ancestry in America. I am speaking of the Spaniards, Portuguese, Italians, Romanians, and others of the Baltic region such as the Croatians. Since the Spanish and Portuguese have been discussed elsewhere in this book and because we can glean wisdom about other Mediterranean and Baltic region members of the White race, this chapter explores the White identity of Italians with a particular focus on the House of Medici—Italy's royalty. As the crude saying went: "Europe ends at Naples. Calabria, Sicily, and all the rest, belong to Africa."[14]

The Italian aristocrats founded their national identities on the idea that their economic and political supremacy was not only providential but necessary for the spread of civilized culture. They did this by developing identities in opposition to Africans, who became the quintessential racial "other" even though many had noted African ancestry.[15]

These falsely based ideologies traveled across the Atlantic well with the emigrants and was reinforced by notions of racism held by White Americans. The denigration of southern Italians and persistence in seeing them as being violent, whether of a revolutionary or criminal action, was upheld. Because of these racist preconceived notions, alarm bells went off when masses of dark-skinned, so-called dirty, ignorant, lazy, subversive, superstitious criminals migrated to the United States and Argentina.

In the United States, a movement developed to halt the Italian's civic participation and restrict their ability to immigrate—this gathered steam and force in the early twentieth century (occurring partially because Italians were the largest group to participate in mass migration in the United States between 1880 and 1920). It should be noted that this vast majority were what were called *contandini* (peasants) and workers coming in search of jobs.

It is equally important to note that not until 1913 did the women come en masse. This means there were 33 years wherein Italian men set up and populated entire communities, undoubtedly through mixing of one type or another in the absence of Italian American women.

EXCLUSIVITY IN RURAL LOUISIANA

Native-born White farmers of Louisiana acted to exclude all so-called outsiders from their associations. In 1914, the White Farmers Association of Ponchatoula specifically forbade membership to Italians or Sicilians, as well as Japanese, Chinese, Mongolian, Asiatic, Asians, Africans, or descendants from "African farmers." Even as immigrants in a New World, the Sicilians and other southern Italians were looked upon as "other" by the larger White community and cast instead as an ethnic minority because of phenotype and known history of racial mixing.

THE SITUATION IN LOUISIANA: SOUTHERN ITALIANS NEITHER BLACK NOR WHITE

Southern Italians have confronted numerous types of discrimination bordering on racism that was ethnically, religiously, and certainly economically motivated. The message came from the Old Country. The Italian government did go so far to protect its former citizens from the fate of many African Americans by petitioning the United States authorities under certain treaty rights to obtain indemnities for Italian nationals involved in wrongful deaths such as through lynching. Yet officials could not claim indemnities for immigrants that did not file for their U.S. citizenship. As the *Crisis,* newspaper of the NAACP (National Association for Colored People) reported, the privilege of American citizenship gave to all African Americans and some Italian immigrants "the inalienable right of every free American citizen to be lynched without recourse or redress."[16]

NEITHER WHITE OR BLACK: IN SEARCH OF COMMUNITY

Italians in Louisiana seemed to occupy a status neither Black nor White, sometimes even denied legal rights given to African Americans. Feeling uncomfortable and unwelcome by their fellow European Americans, often they sought refuge in the Black community wherein they would set up pockets that maintained their strong cultural identity. These groups felt excluded from using certain public facilities like fountains, toilets, and water fountains, but because of the entrepreneurial spirit alive within the Italian communities and ability to own property, they could use these facilities where there was Italian owned and operated property or where they were allowed to by the communities-at-large.

This group of disenfranchised people, particularly Sicilian immigrants in rural Louisiana between 1880 and 1910, worked alongside African Americans mostly on sugar plantations but also strawberry farms and in lumber yards.[17] The two and similar groups shared the same low socioeconomic status as wage laborers in rural industries. Regarded by the longer-standing White society as racially different and socially inferior, Sicilians interacted freely with the Black coworkers while retaining their separate ethnic identity. At the same time, they suffered forms of White violence, terror, and exclusion. Hailing from a country whose own government regarded Sicilians as retarded or inferior, they came all the way to the United States unfortunately only to receive similar discrimination.[18]

BUT AREN'T ITALIANS REALLY WHITE?

Whether Italians are White has been an ongoing debate—they certainly have become so, with all the rights and privileges that go along with it. However, their distant past of trade and enslavement put them into early, intimate contact with people of other races. Moreover, their immigrant experience in the Americas continued to do the same. In Argentina and Brazil, where one-quarter of the Italian population migrated,[19] the mixture was among Americas indigenous groups. In the United States, this already multiracially mixed group of people with Indo-European, sub-Saharan African, and various types of Asiatic ancestry continued to mix with Native Americans, other White people, and to a lesser extent, African Americans. This is healthy.

The multiracial phenomenon, which includes people who self-identify as monoracial, affords an opportunity to challenge the notion of mutually exclusive racial categories, which present the opportunity for racist ideologies and divisive behaviors and conceptions to perpetuate. The opportunity for Italians and other European Americans to identity as multiracial could facilitate a shift—a questioning of the artificially set, stagnant ideas of racial and ethnic categories—more fiction that fact.[20]

BIRACIAL ROYALS: CHALLENGING COMMON CONCEPTIONS

The occurrence and history of biracial and triracial in the Americas is well established. However, when we want to make a racial distinction between White and Black we typically point to Europe's blue-veined royalty when speaking of the White race. Continuing our focus around Italy, examination of its sixteenth-century royal court challenges this commonly held notion, for it is there that the first biracial head of state was born.

Allesandro de Medici was a powerful figure during the early Italian Renaissance. His father was Cardinal Giulio de Medici who later became Pope Clement VII, also nephew of Lorenzo the Magnificent. While Allesandro was born, the child of a Black serving woman, since his father was a member of the elder line of the Medicis, he rose to power though technically he was what would have been called a bastard. Giulio and Giulia his children, took great pride in their Medici ancestry. The two were not only welcomed into Italian society but also married titled individuals.

Today, many noble families of Europe can trace their ancestry back to Alessandro de Medici, the biracial duke of Florence. Scholar Mario de Valdes y Cocom, working through PBS,[21] illustrates that these royal families with African descendants are not limited to Italy but are in several other countries as well. The PBS special also highlights England's Queen Charlotte, wife of King George III, as being someone who descended from the Black Portuguese royal family of Margarita de Castro y Sousa. Her blood line is found in six different lines of European royals.

Margarita de Castro y Sousa

Giulio de Medici, (Allessandro's son) Knight Commander of the Gallery of St. Stephen m. Lucrezia, Countess Gaetani
Cosimo de Medici (illegitimate) m. Lucrezia (II), Countess Gaetani
Angelica de Medici m. Gianpetro, Count Altemps
Maria Cristina, Countess Altemps m. 1646 Ipollito, Duke Lante della Rovere
Antonio, Duke Lante m. 1682 Angelique, Princesse de La Tremouille
Marie Anne Lante m. Jean Baptiste, Duke of Croy Havre
Louis, Duke of Croy Havre m. 1736 Marie Louise, Princess of Montmorency Luxembourg
Joseph, Duke of Croy Havre m. 1762 Adelaide, Princess of Croy Solre
Adelaide, Duchess of Croy Havre m. 1788 Emanuel, Prince of Croy Solre
Constance, Princess of Croy Solre m. 1810 Ferdinand, Duke of Croy
Augusta, Duchess of Croy m. 1836 Alfred, Prince of Salm Salm
Alfred, Prince of Salm Salm m. 1869 Rosa, Countess Lutzow
Emanuel, Prince of Salm Salm m. 1902 Christina von Hapsburg, Archduchess of Austria
Rosemary, Princess of Salm Salm m. 1926 Hubert Salvator von Hapsburg, Archduke of Austria[22]

Another Example of Alessandro's Descent:

Joseph, Duke of Croy Havre m. 1762 Adelaide, Princess of Croy Solre
Amalie, Duchess of Croy Havre m. 1790 Charles, Marquis of Conflans
Amalie de Conflans m. 1823 Eugene, Prince of Ligne
Henri, Prince of Ligne m. 1851 Marguerite, Countess of Talleyrand Perigord
Ernest Louis, Prince of Ligne m. 1887 Diane Marchioness of Cosse Brissac
Eugene, Prince of Ligne m. 1917 Phillipine, Princess Noailles
Yolanda, Princess of Ligne m. 1950 Karl von Hapsburg, Archduke of Austria[23]

Another Example of Alessandro's Descent:

Giulio de Medici, Knight Commander of the Gallery of St. Stephen m. Lucrezia, Countess Gaetani
Cosimo de Medici (illegitimate) m. Lucrezia, Countess Gaetani
Angelica de Medici m. Gianpetro, Count Altemps
Maria Cristina, Countess Altemps m. 1646 Ipollito, Duke Lante della Rovere
Antonio, Duke Lante m. 1682 Angelique, Princesse de La Tremouille
Luigi, Duke Lante m. Angela, Princess Vaini
Fillipo, Duke Lante m. Faustina, Marchioness Caprianca
Maria Christina Lante m. Averado, Duke Salviati
Anna Maria Salviati m. Marcantonio , Prince Borghese
Camillo, Prince Borghese m. 1803 Pauline Bonaparte, Napoleon's Sister[24]

Another Example of Alessandro's Descent:

Marie Anne Lante m. Jean Baptiste, Duke of Croy Havre
Adelaide, Croy Havre m. Emanuel, Prince of Croy Solre
Constance, Princess of Croy Solre m. 1810 Ferdinand of Croy Solre
Juste Marie, Prince of Croy m. 1854 Marie, Countess Ursel
Charles, Prince of Croy m. 1896 Matilda, Countess Robiano
Marie Imaculee m. 1926 Thiery, count of Limburg Stirum
Evrard, Count of Limburg Stirum m. 1957 Helen, Princess of France daughter of the Count of Paris[25]

While some people labor under the impression that to be biracial is not to have a history, the lesson of Alessandro de Medici and Queen Charlotte suggests otherwise. The history of these two and all of their descendants demonstrates that not only do biracial and multiracial people have a history but an illustrious and influential one at that.[26]

TOWARD ETHNOEMPATHY

The acceptance of multiracial identity should eventually change the outlook of European Americans and African Americans, especially when considering the long-standing racial mixing that has occurred in Europe's nobility. In the case of the peasant classes and all in between, greater empathy on the part of others for the experiences of self-identified African Americans could lead to a greater level of identification with—and appreciation of—each other's experiences in what John Cruz coined *ethnoempathy*, undermining the thought process that breeds racism, its categories, and social destruction.[27]

NOTES

1. Rainier Spencer, "Race and Mixed Race: A Personal Tour," in *As We Are Now: Mixedblood Essays on Race and Identity*, ed. William S. Penn (Berkeley: University of California Press, 1997).

2. Maria P. P. Root, *Racially Mixed People of America* (Thousand Oaks, CA: Sage Publishers, 1992), 3–11.

3. F. James Davis, *Who Is Black? One Nation's Definition* (State College, PA: Penn State University Press, 1991).

4. Jayne O. Ifekwunigwe, ed., *Mixed Race Studies: A Reader* (London: Routledge, 2004), 3.

5. Itaberi Njeri, *The Last Plantation: Color, Conflict and Identity: Reflections of a New World Black* (New York: Houghton and Mifflin, 1997), 216–236.

6. Lewis Gordon, *Her Majesties Other Children: Sketches of Racism from a Neocolonial Age* (Latham, MD: Rowman & Littlefield Publishers, 1997), 158.

7. Spencer, "Race and Mixed Race: A Personal Tour."

8. Paul R. Spicknard, Rowena Fong, and Patricia Ewalt, "Undermining, the Very Basis of Racism—Its Categories," *Social Work* (1995): 581–584.

9. Ibid.

10. Quoted in D. J. Dickerson, *The End of Blackness* (New York: Pantheon Books, 2004).

11. Josiah Clark Nott, George Robins Gliddon, "Hybridity of Animals, Viewed in Connection with the Natural History of Mankind," in *Types of Mankind of Ethnological Research* (2854) 373–374 and 396–398.

12. Ibid.

13. Norman Roth, *Conversos, Inquisition and the Expulsion of the Jews from Spain* (Madison: University of Wisconsin Press, 1995).

14. Jennifer Guglielmo and Salvatore Salerno, "White Lies, Dark Truth," in *Are Italians White?: How Race is Made in America*, ed. Jennifer Guglielmo and Salvatore Salerno (New York: Routledge, 2003), 9.

15. Ibid., 10.

16. *The Crisis*, November 1910; letter from Secretary Hay to Count Macchi de Cellere, March 10, 1904, in *Notes to Foreign Legations*, U.S. Department of State.

17. Vincenz Scarpaci, "Walking the Color Line: Italian Immigration in Rural Louisiana 1880–1910" in *Are Italians White?* ed. Jennifer Guglielmo and Salvatore Salerno (New York: Routledge, 2003).

18. Ibid.

19. Donna R. Gabaccia, "Race, Nation, Hyphen: Italian-Americans and American Multiculturalism in Comparative Perspective," in *Are Italians White?* ed. Jennifer Guglielmo and Salvatore Salerno, (New York: Routledge, 2003), 44–46.

20. Ibid.

21. Mario de Valdes y Cocom, "PBS Online: Frontline; Alessandro Medici, Blurred Racial Lines," http://www.pbs.org/wgbh/pages/frontline/shows/secret/famous/medici.html (last accessed July 1, 2008).

22. Ibid.

23. Ibid.

24. Ibid.

25. Ibid.

26. Ibid.

27. Paul R. Spicknard, Rowena Fong, and Patricia Ewalt, "Undermining, the Very Basis of Racism—Its Categories," 581–84.

CHAPTER 7

Black, White, and Red All Over American History: Coming Together yet Remaining Apart

> Many psychologists persist in declaring that there are such things as monoracial identities . . . Mixed race identity or metizajes can be experienced in a variety of ways. It can be ignored, put in context, glorified, denied and, as with race, reified . . . Mestizaje has for me, always been below the surface. As far back as I can remember, I've known I was mixed . . . No, I'm not white, and I don't want to be. Nor am I mixed or black either, for the words are meaningless as predicates the real world. Like unicorn, and flat earth, they describe fantasies, unrealities, wishes. My journey has taken me past constructions of race, past constructions of mixed-race and into an understanding of human difference that does not include race in a meaningful category.
>
> —*Rainier Spencer*[a]
>
> [a] Rainier Spencer, "Race and Mixed Race: A Personal Tour," in *As We Are Now: Mixed Blood Essays on Race and Identity* (anthology), ed. William S. Penn (Berkeley: University of California Press, 1997), 128, 132–134, 137.

FROM NORTH JERSEY TO SOUTH

Shamefully, at times, my mind's eye and memories resort to recording my childhood in Black and White. Sometimes I see and speak a black-and-white filmic history—first growing up in a "Black" suburb of New York in northern New Jersey and then moving at about 7 to a "White" very rural small town in South Jersey—the reality was much more Technicolor than any black-and-white film could suggest.

East Orange, which is where I first lived, and its environs in northern New Jersey was largely comprised of people of color—this much is true. We were African American, West Indian, Jamaican, East Indian, and Puerto Rican. The area also hosts Mediterranean Europeans of Italy and Portugal as well as other White ethnic groups, who all tend to cluster in neighborhood defined groups—Spike Lee brought this type of divided yet parallel community living to life in his very telling movie *Do the Right Thing* (1989).

While, my overriding memory of my North Jersey childhood is "Black," my best friends at the time, the children that shared our building, were clearly multiracial. One with milky-white skin and two honey-brown long braids she could sit on, and the other, the daughter of a first-generation Italian mother and African American father. We shared a three-flat (a three-story apartment building) and many good times together as well as each others cultures, stories, and especially food.

We moved to Salem County in South Jersey, which I saw at the time as White, especially in contrast to East Orange. Yet, it too contains a rich cultural milieu, part of which sparked the inspiration for this book. There was always the Latino presence, though unlike here in Chicago, where that presence is predominately Mexican American, there were Puerto Ricans in South Jersey drawn to possibilities of working in the profusion of farming industries that cover the area. Using my personal experiences and upbringing as a cultural backdrop, this chapter explores triracial and Black Indian relationships in and around the areas of my kin—New Jersey through Virginia.

PARADISE LAKES

The actual neighborhood we lived in was founded by a Philadelphia A.M.E. (African Methodist Episcopal) church as a resort town; thus it was fittingly named Paradise Lakes. In the book *The Color Complex* by Kathy Russell, Midge Wilson, and Ronald Hall, it is described as the earliest church in America established exclusively for Negroes, founded in 1703 in Philadelphia.[1] Most of the founders were upper-middle-class African Americans involved with the community of faith, teachers, doctors, and investors, and most were landowners. It was a community at the time open to the GLBT (gay, lesbian, bisexual, and transgendered) community, Blacks, Whites, and people of multiethnic heritage, much unlike the town of Alloway itself, in which it was situated, which at the time was segregated. We were at that time the so-called colored enclave and were not allowed to live any closer than the five miles we stayed from the town center.

Still, many of us labor as I did as a child, under the impression that we are living in a Black, White, brown, red, or yellow neighborhood, but if we look realistically at all those we interact with, we begin to see, even within these seemingly monoracial communities that there is a subtle rainbow. Taking a walk with one of my girlfriends, comparing and contrasting notes on where and how each of us grew up, I came to this realization—I grew up in a very culturally rich stew.

WHAT'S YOUR NAME?

At church, which was predominately African American, we also had parishioners with names such as Drains, Driggs, Pierce, Cuff, Moore, Hammond, Harmon, Valentine, Denby, and Dunn. So what's in a surname? These particular names are associated with various bands of the remnant groups of the Delaware Indians and were heavily triracially mixed. Some appeared entirely White, and some were very dark-skinned—all sat together on the stiff wooden pews, worshipping under one roof, in an otherwise racially divided area.

These surnames belong to South Jersey's triracial people, though they can be found farther south and east as well. Some identify as Native Americans, part of remnant tribes of the Delaware such as the Mitsawoket; others are called Goulds or are simply called by their surname as representative of their particular triracial blend.

In fact, South Jersey when I was growing up was a microcosm, if you are at all interested in triracial isolates, mixed-raced, or multicultural identity.

GOULDTOWN

Directly due south and east of Paradise Lakes lies a very intriguing town. According to the February 1952 *Ebony* articles on Gouldtown, it was at the time the oldest Negro settlement of freedmen in the United States at 250 years old (it is now over 300 years of age). Light-skinned descendants of the original settlers continue to live there largely as farmers. This five mile square town, 40 miles from Philadelphia was established by the granddaughter of John Fenwick (New Jersey's founder) and a Black man surnamed Gould. Despite derision, disdain, hatred and attempts to disgrace them, the two defied their times, married, had numerous children whose descendants continue to thrive there. According to the article, most Goulds in the United States can trace their lineage back to this interracial couple. There are five principle family surnames of Gouldtown—Pierce, Murray, Cuff, and Wright, as well, of course, Gould.[a]

---

[a] *Ebony* magazine, February 1952, http://www.mitsawokett.com/MoorsOfDelaware/Ebony1952-LargeImage.htm (accessed July 7, 2008).

On the one hand, Blacks and Whites were largely segregated, yet there were rainbow people in my school and churches; call them tan, if you will, but they were a clear visual indicator that we were not monocultural people—nor strictly sticking to one side or another, consisting of pure races. Some acted as bridges, at ease among those of us who identified as African Americans, while others stayed to themselves in their own communities even, for example living in Gouldtown—the triracial-exclusive community we just explored.

What I saw were that some of these folks were white skinned but had thick, wavy "Black" hair, whereas others were the faintest tan, while others still were dark brown-skinned with straight or wavy hair—most were perfectly at home with those of us who identify as African Americans. Others more golden skinned and fair haired with so-called negroidal features, more properly an African phenotype, stayed more to themselves in places like Gouldtown, whereas hundreds of others who could "pass" melted into the European American community only exhibiting the faintest reflection of their prior "Negro" or "colored" identity.

Several aunts from different sides of the family married, rather difficultly it would seem, into these rather insular families. My Aunt Edith for example, my mother's sister, married Henry Dunn, a Mitsawoket, after feeling the wrath of his children. My family and I were taken aback, knowing our family was already multiracial, indeed our grandfather was biracial and so was his mother. Moreover, my aunt and uncle-to-be were past child-bearing age. Apparently, there was deep concern that the family would be ousted from their tribal status and that perhaps my uncle would not be able to buried on tribal grounds. The couple did marry, and their greatest fears did not come to pass.

Meanwhile, we gained a treasure in an uncle, someone who was open, warm, loving, and accepting to our entire family. My father, grandfather, and Uncle Henry became very close, often fishing and swapping stories on the dock. Interestingly, my father's step-grandfather was a full-blooded Cherokee Indian from the Foster family, and I believe Uncle Henry became a surrogate for that cherished experience he had as a child because both men were influential as mentors to him. Uncle Henry quickly became one of our favorite uncles and an ambassador for what heretofore had been a mystery people to most of us.

Ruddy skinned with pin-straight, snow-white hair, he and the aunt who was like a grandmother to me were inseparable until the end of their lives. It was difficult and remains so to this day to understand the mind-set of his family. Why was there so much antipathy and so many road blocks thrown up in the way of such a fortuitous union of two widowers? To understand this we need to delve into the very dense, tangled, sometimes troubled waters that are the history of the triracial triangle.

THE MITSAWOKETT OF CENTRAL DELAWARE THROUGH SOUTH JERSEY

During the 1600s, the documented chief (*sachem*) between St. Jones and Duck Creek, Kent County, Delaware was Christian. His Indian name was Petticoquewan. He was sachem of a band called the Mitsawokett, most likely remnants that continue to be reflected in the present-day mixed-blood Native American East Coast communities.

It may be due to their low visibility and geographic distribution that they have been counted as "free Blacks" during the antebellum period. Ned Heite's study shows conclusively that "Free Persons of Color" were not always Negro and that mulatto cannot be taken to only mean African ancestry.[a]

There is good evidence that large numbers of Indians stayed behind during each "removal" episode. To this day, there are remnant communities in each of the steps along the westward migration. Indians living in New Jersey, New York, Pennsylvania, and Delaware from the time of contact through the 1700s were forcibly removed from their land or fled to avoid brutalization. Some dissolved into European American and African American communities temporarily losing their Indian identities or gaining a new one, depending on how you look at it.

The Mitsawokett believe their ancestors left many orally transmitted records, letting them know they are descended from one or the other of the Lenni-Lennape and Nanticoke peoples of the Delmarva area. Considered the "Grandfather People" to many tribes, the Delaware Lenni Lennape, or "true men," originally lived in New York, Delaware, New Jersey, and Pennsylvania, and many still do.

---

[a] Dr. Louise Heite, *Heite Consulting's Reports: Delaware's Invisible Indians.* http://www.mitsawokett.com/HeiteReport1.htm (accessed May 15, 2008).

THE BLACKFOOT QUESTION

When asking of my ethnic identity from my earliest memories, I recall being told we were part Native American. Of course my anthropological mind wanted to know more. Which people, how many different types, where did they live, who were these ancestors? I was told "Cherokee" and indeed our family surnames do match up to both the eastern band of Cherokee and the Chickasaws. However, my maternal grandmother would also get a big kick out of saying we were Blackfoot 'cause of our "nigger toes" but would never go into any convincing details.

Many African Americans who have family stories that include a Native American ancestor will point to the Blackfoot as the possible tribal identification. Though at first I thought geography excluded the possibility of very many (if any) African Americans actually being of Blackfoot ancestry, further research confirmed that it would be rare but not impossible for African Americans to be related to the Blackfoot—particularly the eastern band also called Saponi.

THE SAPONI

The Saponi are one of the eastern Siouan tribes, formerly living in North Carolina and Virginia, and occasionally included Tutelo people. Sapon was a town of the Tutelo confederacy on a tributary of upper Roanoke village or Otter River. The people moved apart and settled near Occaneechi, each group occupying its own island. They eventually sought refuse in Virginia and made a new settlement before the Tuscarora War of 1711 called Sapona town. These groups of people are believed to be a large contributing stock to today's triracial, multiracial, and Indian remnant communities of the central East Coast.

THE BLACKFOOT OF THE DAKOTAS

The Blackfoot were referred to as such because of their distinctive black moccasins, not because they were darker skinned. The Blackfoot people are thought to have been always concentrated in the Dakotas, whereas the majority of African Americans were found in the southern states. However, there are no hard-and-fast rules for either group. Still, some freed African American slaves did resettle in the West and a few may have mixed with the Blackfoot. While, it is little noted, numerous biracial (Black/Indians) were forced to resettle in the West along with full-blooded American Indians on the Trail of Tears. There is a possibility of some cultural blends occurring from the Trail of Tear migration. Support is thin in this area; however, there are numerous Black Indian groups who could assist one doing such a search. One of the more prominent online sites is administered by Angela Walton-Raji and is called the African-Native American Genealogy Web site (http://www.african-nativeamerican.com; the forum to ask questions and converse is located at http://www.afrigeneas.com/forume/index.cgi?#m_28895).

BATTLING: TO KEEP INDIAN-NESS IN, "OTHERS" MUST BE RULED OUT

Since the first explorers set foot on what has come to be known as American soil, the relationship between people of Native, European, and African descent has been charged. Depending on who is recording this intense, sometimes unwanted immersion, the story and its components differ greatly. It has been a badge of honor in current times, most recently to have Native American heritage, but Native Americans' feelings about having White or Black blood, as I indicated through the personal story of my Aunt Edith and Uncle Henry, is far more complex.

At the same time as the French and Indian War, but not connected to it, there was a significant change developing concerning race in America. There was a tougher attitude toward people of African descent. Concurrently, there was growing support for the abolitionist movement, particularly strong in the Quaker Community of the East and Southeast. Yet, the economic importance of slavery made those involved with benefiting from it all the more dedicated to maintaining the practice of slavery, keeping everyone with a drop of African blood enslaved.

This strained what was already a complex relationship between American Blacks and American Indians. From early on, runaway slaves and indentured servants found refuge in Native American nations. Similarities in hunting, fishing, farming, and agricultural techniques were marked between the Native Americans and African-descended people brought here. At the same time, it must be noted that White runaways, indentured servants, and the like, also ran off and were said to have "gone Indian."

Racially ambiguous communities sometimes referred to as isolates or triracial or triracial isolate communities are found throughout the United States, particularly in the upper South.[2]

BLACK, WHITE, AND RED, ALL OVER AMERICAN HISTORY

Surviving Native Americans, or remnant groups as they are sometimes referred to, for the most part, live outside federally recognized groups and not on reservations. More than a hundred distinct Indian remnant groups lack recognition by the Department of the Interior. Without tribal recognition, these groups have faced many economic, political, and social issues that challenges their tribal identity. The non-reservation Indians' descendants from removed tribes of the East Coast probably number 120,000.

MULATTOES: A BROADER DEFINITION

The term *mulatto* in particular was taken to mean anyone dark skinned who was not Negro. In the West Indies this was already applied to the Black-Indian admixed groups as well as to those who were half-Christian and half another religion.[a]

[a] Edward Heite, *Delaware's Invisible Indians, Part II* (Camden, DE: Heite Consulting, 2005), 3.

Many Indians of the East are there because their ancestors deliberately renounced Native American culture during removal. Those groups of Indians that chose to maintain their traditional ways of life were pushed off their lands. Others who stayed adapted as quickly as possible. Because it was not prudent to be called Indian, they allowed themselves to be listed as Negro, colored, or mulatto until 1830, when mixed communities were pretty much left to their own devices.

Powhatan Timeline

1520—The coastal Indians of Virginia first encountered European explorers.
1584—The first English colonists arrived in North America at Roanoke Islands, North Carolina.
1590—John White, the colony leader, returned from England to find the Roanoke Colony deserted.
1607—First English colony to survive in North America was established but nearly abandoned in 1610. However, more colonists arrived, and it began to thrive.
1609—Powhatan abandoned Werowocomoco, which was 45 acres of land.
1612—First coordinated attempt by the Powhatan to expel the settlers, led by Opechancanough, Wahunsunacok's brother, the last of the Powhatan to exert control.
1613—Pocahontas (in English), was kidnapped.
1614—A treaty between her father and the colonists was struck; she converted to Christianity. Married John Wolfe.
1615—Thomas Rolfe, son of Pocahontas and John Wolfe, was born.
. . . Later

- The Rappahannock tribe lost its reservation in 1700.
- The Chickahominy lost their reservation in 1718.
- The Nansemond sold their reservation in 1792.
- The Gingaskin (Accomac) Reservation on the Eastern Shore subdivided in 1813; pressured, they sold their land by 1850.
- Miraculously, the Pamunkey, Mattaponi of the Eastern Shores kept their reservations. Triracial groups such as the Melungeon previously trace their Native American ancestry to the Pamunkey, Mattaponi, and other groups of the former Powhatan confederacy.

THE POWHATAN

For the Indians have also been assimilated and lost in the White population. The process began when the Jamestown Colony, sent by Virginia Company, established itself largely through the romantic marriage in 1613 of John Rolfe with Princess Pocahontas, daughter of Emperor Powhatan, who ruthlessly ruled the eastern seaboard. Certain Virginia families proudly claim descent. In fact, the hybrids of those early days form the foundations of America's old aristocracy.

—Cedric Dover[3]

Led by Captain John Smith, settlers explored surrounding area of James, York, Rappahannock to the Potomac River and fall line. Smith published a coastal plain map. Smith and other settlers encountered the Powhatan.

Powhatan refers to the Algonquian speakers of Virginia's tide-water region. Most of the region was under leadership of one *weroance*[4] (high chief) named Wahunsunacock. Later, he took the name Powhatan, after his birth town. At English contact, Native Tidewater population was 2,000; Powhatan controlled 32 chiefdoms and 150 settlements. People paid tributes and taxes in the form of game and produce to Powhatan. In return, Powhatan fed his people from his reserves and provided protection.

Meanwhile, hundreds of towns and villages were built. Powhatan begins to be marginalized and pushed, so his people begin moving farther inland. The Powhatan settled as agrarians, fishing, hunting, and foraging. Powhatan appealed to Captain Smith in 1609, meeting at Werowocomoco, his headquarters. Werowocomoco is a Native American village along the Puritan Bay at York River, Gloucester County, Virginia, which dates back to the late woodland period of 900–1607, and early contact was 1607–1609. The site represents the sole location where Powhatan and Captain Smith met in person.[5]

Eventually, the once mighty Powhatan chiefdom was reduced to tributary status. It lost all lands between the York and Black Water rivers. In 1677 another treaty was made. Indians on the coast lost all the rest of their land and were confined to reservations. By the 1800s, after non-Indians poured into the territories formerly settled by Virginia's Indian populations, Native American languages were rarely heard except for Siouan Tutelo.[6]

CHICKAHOMINY TRIBE

The Chickahominy Tribe lived along the Chickahominy River from the James River to the middle of current county of New Kent. Chickahominy are Algonquin speakers that lived in North Carolina and Virginia at the first contact. They were basically independent, though allied with the Powhatan confederacy. They had eight Mangai (great men/leaders), 200–250 warriors, and 600–900 people in many villages along the lower Chickahominy River.

They had early contact with Jamestown. The Chickahominy sided with the English colonists' treaty of 1614, which provided for 300 Chickahominy warriors to fight the Spaniards. The eight Mangai were regarded as noblemen of King James. Still, the Chickahominy republic was ravaged during raids of 1623–1627. They later moved to King William County. Forced from their reservation in 1718, they settled near the Mattaponi Reservation, but that was lost to the English as well. Tribal families began to gradually migrate, leading back to Kent County and Charles City County. Originally, villages known as Chickahominy Ridge halfway between

SIDE BAR: CHICKAHOMINY EASTERN DIVISION

The Chickahominy Eastern Division split off from the Chickahominy after a disagreement regarding land development. In 1921 the New Kent Country band organized its own tribe. In 1922 they founded their church, Tsena Commocko Indian Baptist, outside Providence Forge. They built a school, incorporated in 1935, and were recognized by state of Virginia in 1983. They are located in New Kent County, 25 miles east of Richmond, Virginia, with a tribal membership of about 150 people.[a]

[a] Chickahominytribe.org Eastern Division, http://www.cied.org (accessed October 15, 2008).

Richmond and Williamsburg established Samaria Baptist Church, which is still a functioning focal point. They purchased a tribal center and host powwows. The Chickahominy use an election process to select chiefs. It is one of Virginia's largest state-recognized tribes and has a board of directors.[7]

THE PAMUNKEY

The Pamunkey Indians were the most powerful of the tribes in the great Powhatan paramount chiefdom, which consisted of 35 tribes, approximately 10,000 people under the leadership of Powhatan. The Pamunkey occupied a 1,200-acre island-like peninsula on the Pamunkey River that comprises their current reservation, uninterrupted since precolonial times, located in King William County. After 10,000 acres were ceded to William and Mary College, they could no longer sustain themselves off the land, and thus the Pamunkey took up more modern farming techniques. While considered a triracial mixed community by some, the Pamunkey have tenaciously maintained a distinctly tribal identity that centers around the land. They live in houses and mobile homes scattered about their farms on the reservation with surrounding forested hunting that is shared.

CHEROENHAKA (NOTTOWAY) AND MEHERIN

Two distinct groups, the Cheroenhaka (also called the NA-DA-WA or Nottoway) and Meherin, also lived in the plains of Virginia. The Cheroenhaka (Nottoway), the Meherin, and the Tuscarora were the three main Iroquoian-speaking tribes living east of the fall line on the inner coastal plains of southeastern Virginia.[8] They spoke a form of the Iroquoian languages and lived near the Nottoway and Meherin rivers. They farmed and hunted. Their houses were similarly interspersed among their cultivated crops. The Cheroenhaka and Meherin lived as autonomous groups with a local chief. They had their first ethno-historic contact with the English between 1607 and1608. They remained relatively undisturbed by Jamestown settlers, but by 1650, the fur trade increased contact.[9] James Edward Bland encountered two Cheroenhaka Indian villages, Chounteroute Town governed by Chounteroute, king of the Nottoways, and Tonnatorah, south of the side of the Nottoway River where the current Sussex-Greenville County line meets the River. The tribal name Cheroenhaka means "People at the Fork of the Stream."[10]

In a 1677 treaty, they lost their rights, becoming tributaries to their colonies. They set up reservations along Nottoway River, Southampton County. In the late 1700s, the Meherin lost their reservation, but the Nottoway held on to theirs. Today, the Nottoway are officially recognized by five southeastern Virginia counties.

By 1722, many southeastern tribes met their demise or were absorbed by other cultures. The Nottoway formed what are known as modern citizen tribes, consisting of composite tribes such as the remnants of the Chickahominy, Upper Mattaponi, and Rappahannock. The Nottoway subdivided in 1878; many families have held their land since.[11]

THE RAPPAHANNOCK

The Rappahannock had initial contact with Captain Smith at 1608 at their King Towne, Cat Point Creek, and at that time they had 13 settlements on the south side of the river and 2 on north side. Around 1705, they were driven off their land and relocated to 3,474-acre reservation at Indian Neck in King and Queen Col, located on traditional winter hunting grounds between the Mattaponi and Rappahannock rivers. Triracial descendants of the Rappahannock have remained there until the present day. They incorporated in 1921 with the state of Virginia and were officially recognized as one of the historic tribes of the commonwealth of Virginia in 1983. There are about 300 members, and they maintain their own cultural center and museum. Today's generation of the Rappahannock maintain their heritage by teaching younger members crafts and educating about the history of the tribe. Their dance group is quite popular and is called the Rappahannock Indian Dancers. They can be reached at rappahannocktrib@aol.com.

THE FIVE CIVILIZED TRIBES

While the term "The Five Civilized Tribes" casts aspersion on tribes outside this group, the term is widely used so, I will employ it here though I don't agree with it. Genealogical documentation connects African Americans definitively to the so called five civilized tribal groups: Cherokee,

Choctaw, Chickasaw, Creek and Seminole. Historically there have been additional admixtures with the most prominent being the:

Chickahominy, Gingaskin, Mattaponi, Nansemond, Nanticoke, Nottaway, Pamunkey, Rappahannocks, Saponi, Weanock and Werowocomo people.

THE NANTICOKE

Furthermore, there were American Indian peoples throughout the Southeast in the early days, and with these the Negroes mingled to a degree that Whites usually fail to recognize, though to a Negro, knowledge of Indian ancestry is generally a matter of pride. This mingling also took place in the West Indies, whence came many of those that later formed part of the American Negro community.

The Nanticoke, who still live in Canada, are a dark-skinned tribe of African and Indian descent. In the *Ebony* magazine article "*Black Indians Hit Jackpot in Casino Bonanza,*" author Kevin Chappell reports on a similar tribe of Black Indians in America.

According to Chappell, the Mashantucket Pequot Indian tribe of Connecticut owns the most profitable casino in the world. Last year they took in $800 million.[12] It is this fact that has brought them to international public attention. Confusion arises for the public that harbors preconceptions of what "Indian" means and what it looks like. The Mashantucket have about 318 members, half of whom could pass for Black. Their Foxwood Resort Casino is located in a sedate community in southeastern Connecticut called Ledyard. Remote location aside, they have raised the eyebrows of Donald Trump, who calls them "Michael Jordan Indians" because they seem to him to be African Americans and not Native Americans.

THE PEQUOTS

While its members enjoy relative comfort because of their successful business venture today, they were nearly annihilated 350 years ago. The Pequots were massacred 300 years ago and enslaved along with Africans, with whom they intermarried. By the 1970s, this group was a shadow of its former self, with only two half-sister members to represent the tribe. Two is indeed a small number for a nation; the sisters were feisty and held fast to the 216 acres of Pequot land. Gradually, descendants returned to the reservation, and the numbers were replenished.

Currently, the Pequot are not only successful as a sound culture with a solid economic standing, but they are also a model for diversity in a pluralistic America. Dark-skinned and light-skinned members may suggest an African or European heritage, but the tribe is united as Pequot people, a rainbow tribe. This group with lengthy American roots and a venerable history teaches important lessons to contemporary Americans. The resilience of the Pequot proves that connection to a place and a common history creates a bond more important than physical characteristics.

NOTES

1. Kathy Russell, Midge Wilson, and Ronald Hall, *The Color Complex: The Politics of Skin Color Among African Americans* (New York: Anchor Books/Random House, 1993), 27.

2. Ibid., 2.

3. Cedric Dover, *Half-Caste* (London: Secker and Warburg, 1937), 203–211.

4. *Weroance* is an Algonquian word meaning tribal chief, leader, commander, or king notably among the Powhatan confederacy of the Virginia Coastal and Chesapeake Bay people. *Weroansqua* is the feminine form (spellings vary widely).

5. John Smith, *A Map of Virginia* (Oxford: Joseph Barnes, 1612), http://etext.lib.virginia.edu/etcbin/jamestown-browse?id = J1008 (accessed July 7, 2008).

6. Virginia Council of Indians, http://indians.vipnet.org/ (accessed November 14, 2008).

7. Chickahominy Tribe, http://www.chickahominytribe.org (accessed July 5, 2008).

8. Chief Walt "Red Hawk" Brown, "Ethno-Historical Snapshot of the Cheroenhaka (Nottoway) Indian Tribe," http://www.cheroenhaka-nottoway.org/nottoway-history/snap-shot.htm (accessed July 7, 2008).

9. Ibid.

10. Ibid.

11. Virginia Council On Indians, 22 May 2003, Commonwealth of Virginia, Richmond, 20/1/05, http://indians.vipnet.org (accessed August 1, 2008).

12. Kevin Chappell, "Black Indians Hit Jackpot in Casino Bonanza," *Ebony* (June 1995): 46.

CHAPTER 8

The Stolen Generations: When Things Really Go Wrong

> The social construction of race and racism is dependent on the general acceptance of rigid racial boundaries and racial classification systems. Proponents of racial segregation have always understood that interracial relationships and the children they produce eventually undermine racism by challenging the assumption of monolithic, fixed, and inherently incompatible races. The clear demarcation of races, which is an essential cornerstone of the social construction of race, is weakened by the existence and recognition of widespread racial mixing. Consequently, those who favor racial separatism and believe in the concept of race are most likely to strongly oppose interracial relationships.[a]
>
> [a] Richard J. Payne, *Getting Beyond Race: The Changing American Culture.* (Boulder, CO: Westview Press, 1998), 153.

From afar, it is reasonable to presume that mixed-raced people had advantages over mono-racial people historically, particularly those of Indian or Black heritage, who could then escape the stigma and adverse legislation associated with belonging entirely to either group. Though the heritage may have been mixed, society worked rather vigorously to assign people to groups to fit their own desires.

In early America, many mixed-raced people were deemed "Free People of Color," and there were "Freed Men," as well, who were descended from

Africa. There were countless intercultural stressors and disputes resulting from the nebulous boundaries caused by such terminology, law or not.

Free African Americans were also in danger of having their children stolen and sold into slavery. In his Revolutionary War pension application on March 7, 1834, Drury Tann declared in Southampton County, Virginia, Court:

he was stolen from his parents as a boy by strangers, who were carrying him to sell him into Slavery, and had gotten with him and other stolen property as far as the Mountains on their way, that his parents made complaint to a Mr. Tanner Alford who was Then a magistrate in the county of Wake State of North Carolina to get me back from Those who had stolen me and he did pursue the Rogues & overtook Them at the mountains and took me from Them.[1]

An advertisement in the April 10, 1770, issue of the *North Carolina Gazette of New Bern* describes how the Driggers family (a known triracial/ multiracial surname) was victimized in Craven County, North Carolina:

broke into the house . . . under the care of Ann Driggus, a free negro woman, two men in disguise, with marks on their faces, and clubs in their hands, beat and wounded her terribly and carried away four of her children.[2]

And John Scott, "freeborn negro," testified in Berkeley County, South Carolina, on January 17, 1754 that three men, Joseph Deevit, William Deevit, and Zachariah Martin

entered by force, the house of his daughter, Amy Hawley, and carried her off, with her six children, and he thinks they are taking them north to sell as slaves.[3]

One of the children was recovered in Orange County, North Carolina, where the county court appointed Thomas Chavis to return the child to South Carolina on March 12, 1754.[4]

Stealing free African Americans and selling them into slavery in another state was legal in North Carolina until 1779. The law did give a thin veil of protection to Blacks and "coloreds." In 1793, the murderer of John James of Northampton County was committed to jail according to the March 20, 1793, issue of the *North Carolina Journal:*

Last night Harris Allen, who was committed for the murder of John James, a free mulatto, of Northampton County, made his escape from the gaol of this town. He is a remarkable tall man, and had on a short round jacket.[5]

THE STOLEN GENERATIONS OF AUSTRALIA

The damage to families and communities that occurs when families are broken is hard to estimate. One of the most egregious infractions on the rights of biracial children ended in the late part of the twentieth century in Australia. Far away from the rest of this discussion geographically, the story of the "Stolen Generations" of Australia is nevertheless, instructive.

Zita Wallace still remembers the coarse texture of the blanket that she huddled under in anxiety and confusion on the day she was wrenched from her Aboriginal family and sent to live in an orphanage run by white people. It was 1947 and she was seven years old.

"We were put in a dormitory that had mattresses on the floor," she recalls, brushing away flies in the sweltering midday heat of the outback.

She adds: "There were no sheets but we had blankets, like the blankets they used for horses, hairy and rough. They gave us bread and tea and when the sun started to go down we all got upset. I remember little Barbie crying because she was only four and one of the older girls holding her, and walking around with her. I lay down and put the blanket over my head and I was just crying and crying."[6,7]

For over 100 years, between the 1860s and1970s, mixed-race Aborigines and Torres Strait Islander people of Australia were confiscated like illegal contraband, then placed in group homes similar in spirit to internment camps. Many of these centers were religious outposts operated by Catholic nuns. The government of Australia oversaw the program and had a plan of selectively breeding mixed-raced children so that their offspring would become increasingly White.

There were so-called training programs to *civilize* the natives and those of mixed race. Though one might hope training would be educational and offer a wide variety of opportunities the training programs prepared the mixed-race children to work as housekeepers, maids and other service types of domestic jobs to benefit certain White Australian's lifestyles.

The avid collection of biracial children broke many Australian Aboriginal homes, upsetting the unity of entire communities. In desperation to keep the children in their rightful homes, mothers and grandmothers sometimes placed the children over open fires to darken their skin or rubbed charcoal over their bodies to blacken them. Some interracial families lived in exile, in the roughest parts of the outback, to keep others from noticing their multiracial appearance.

Survivors and their families have been fighting legally for many years seeking official apologies from the government, and some are seeking reparations. While many Aboriginal and Torres Strait Islanders now have their own land or countries, those taken from their homes still suffer disproportionately. For example, high percentages of the "Stolen Generations" suffer from depression. Some result to a life of crime; 90 percent of incarcerated Aborigines in Victoria are members of the "Stolen Generations."

Australia's Aboriginal people number about 450,000 of Australia's population of 21 million. They are the poorest ethnic group and are generally most likely to be jailed, unemployed, illiterate, and suffer from poor health. Their life expectancy is 17 years shorter than other Australians.

THE IMPACT OF THE *BRINGING THEM HOME* REPORT

According to the *Bringing Them Home* report (1997), approximately 100,000 Aboriginal children were removed from their parents over several generations. One out of three indigenous children was stolen away between 1910 and 1970, though the heinous activity began as early as the 1860s. While some children were given voluntarily, most were forcibly removed from their parents and community. In 2007, Bruce Trevorrow became the first Aboriginal man to win compensation for these actions from the government. The 1997 *Bringing Them Home* report sparked apologies from state parliaments, but Prime Minister John Howard had refused to offer a public, governmental apology. However, within days of winning November's general elections, the new Australian government of Prime Minister Kevin Rudd promised to formally say sorry to Australia's so-called Stolen Generations.[8]

Poverty is pervasive in these populations as is lack of higher education and the opportunity it affords. As a result of poor role models and lack of contact with real family, the Stolen Generations have more difficulty than others with raising their own families. Unfortunately, lack of self-esteem, feelings of being unworthy, suicidal tendencies, violence, juvenile delinquency, alcohol and drug abuse, as well as personality disorders, have high incidence in this group.

LESSONS LEARNED

There is an important lesson to be learned from the "Stolen Generations."

- Contrary to the Victorian belief that a child inherits culture almost entirely from their mother, a child, no matter how diverse her background may be, still identifies most strongly with both of her parents, her extended family, and the community in which she grows up.
- People of mixed heritage cannot be forced to become fully one race or another if they are of mixed heritage; trying to do so brings psychological harm and breeds social problems within the individual and community.
- Racial identification is best decided by the individual and his or her parents.
- When a society, government, or agency assigns race or cultural orientation of mixed-race children, there are numerous negative psychological and sociological implications that afflict individuals and the community at large.

RECOVERY

As part of a recovery program, concerted efforts are being made to offer therapy, some of it including Aboriginal ritual and ceremony, to help the Stolen Generations heal. Governmental agencies are attempting to help these mixed-raced descendants of Australian Aborigines trace their genealogy and reunite with their traditional family communities in Aboriginal country.

THE APOLOGY

We all wish that those that have wronged us politically, socially, or psychologically would apologize formally. This is something sought by the American Indians and by African Americans who are descendants of the enslaved. Australia has stepped forward to apologize formally for the ill-conceived the laws that allowed entire generations to become stolen from their community based on the fact that they were biracial. The first national Sorry Day was celebrated March 10, 2008.

Prime minister Kevin Rudd used the word *sorry* three times in the historic, 360-word statement read to parliament in the national capital of Canberra on February 13, 2008. He said there came a time in history when people had to reconcile the past with their future.[9]

APOLOGY TO THE STOLEN GENERATIONS

Below is the actual wording of the federal Parliament of Australia's full apology to the Stolen Generations:

Today we honour the Indigenous peoples of this land, the oldest continuing cultures in human history.

We reflect on their past mistreatment.

We reflect in particular on the mistreatment of those who were Stolen Generations – this blemished chapter in our nation's history.

The time has now come for the nation to turn a new page in Australia's history by righting the wrongs of the past and so moving forward with confidence to the future.

We apologise for the laws and policies of successive Parliaments and governments that have inflicted profound grief, suffering and loss on these our fellow Australians.

We apologise especially for the removal of Aboriginal and Torres Strait Islander children from their families, their communities and their country.

For the pain, suffering and hurt of these Stolen Generations, their descendants and for their families left behind, we say sorry.

To the mothers and the fathers, the brothers and the sisters, for the breaking up of families and communities, we say sorry.

And for the indignity and degradation thus inflicted on a proud people and a proud culture, we say sorry.

We the Parliament of Australia respectfully request that this apology be received in the spirit in which it is offered as part of the healing of the nation.

For the future we take heart; resolving that this new page in the history of our great continent can now be written.

We today take this first step by acknowledging the past and laying claim to a future that embraces all Australians.

A future where this Parliament resolves that the injustices of the past must never, never happen again.

A future where we harness the determination of all Australians, Indigenous and non-Indigenous, to close the gap that lies between us in life expectancy, educational achievement and economic opportunity.

A future where we embrace the possibility of new solutions to enduring problems where old approaches have failed.

A future based on mutual respect, mutual resolve and mutual responsibility.

A future where all Australians, whatever their origins, are truly equal partners, with equal opportunities and with an equal stake in shaping the next chapter in the history of this great country, Australia."[10]

LOOKING FORWARD TO HEALING

The history of mixed-race people in the Americas, Spain, Portugal, Italy, South Africa and West Africa, Australia, and beyond is rife with pain. It is a rich and colorful history to be sure, but it has left deep scars. Recognizing our history is important, yet maintaining a healthy focus on the present is even more vital. This chapter ends in the spirit of the Australian apology—a spirit of reconciliation, forgiveness, and looking forward to the future as a collective group of people. It is important to envision a time when our various cultures and their blends are sustainable and holistically healthy. This is just as important, if not more so, than looking back and reawakening our wounds.

NOTES

1. Revolutionary War pension application on 7 March 1834, Drury Tann.
2. Fouts, *NC Gazette of New Bern*, November 14, 1778, I:65–6.
3. John Scott, "freeborn negro," testified in Berkeley County, South Carolina, on January 17, 1754.
4. Haun, Orange County Court Minutes, Craven County Court, Virginia, June 21, 1745 I:70–71.
5. Fouts, *NC Journal*, March 20, 1793, I:205
6. Barbara McMahon "Snatched from Home for a Racist Ideal. Now a Nation says Sorry," (Alice Springs, AU), *The Guardian*, February 11, 2008, http://www.guardian.co.uk/world/2008/feb/11/australia (accessed July 8, 2008).
7. Ibid.
8. "AUSTRALIA: Date Set for Formal 'Stolen Generation' Apology," http://www.radioaustralia.net.au/programguide/stories/200801/s2151634.htm (accessed July 8, 2008).

9. "Kevin Rudd's National Apology to Stolen Generations," February 13, 2008, http://www.news.com.au/story/0,23599,23206140–2,00.html (accessed July 8, 2008).

10. Prime Minister Kevin Rudd, *Australian Apology,* February 13, 2008. Transcript available at http://www.cnn.com/2008/WORLD/asiapcf/02/12/australia.text/index.html (accessed October 23, 2008).

CHAPTER 9

Profiles of Triumph and Courage

TO OUR FUTURE: IMPORTANT NEWSMAKERS OF THE PAST AND PRESENT

Barack Obama

Of course, by the printing of this book, new and wonderful developments will have occurred concerning biracial, triracial, multiethnic, multiracial, and multiculturalism in general. At the writing of this book, one of the most exciting developments has been the election of the first biracial President of the United States, the Senator from Illinois, Barack Obama.[1] Barack Obama has had a meteoric rise on the national scene and hopefully has forever changed how race will be discussed in America and beyond.

Says one journalist:

> he made himself black. But at the very moment he attained his goal, he also transcended it. Obama had too much integrity to believe that "blackness" in itself meant anything, so he simultaneously became black and something irreducible to color. By so doing, he kept faith both with his fellow American blacks, who have been forced by racism to consider their own color as a constituent part of their identity, and also with people of all races.
>
> The essence of Obama's politics, his call for reconciliation and unity, is thus deeply grounded in the long and painful creation of his own double identity. It is, almost literally, sealed in blood—the mixed blood, black and white, that flows in his veins. With Obama, the movement is always toward a double affirmative. Not neither black nor white, which is the way I and many mixed-race people identify ourselves, but both black and something larger.
>
> —Gary Kamiya[2]

His sweeping calls for hope and anthem forged around change have been the winning combination that led to his becoming the nominee for the Democratic nomination for president of the United States in 2008. A man with a distinctively bicultural background (living in Hawaii, Kansas, Chicago, and Indonesia) and biracial as well as bicultural heritage (Kenyan father, White American mother), he has brought these issues into the national discussion—from cable television's punditocrasy to spectators' stands filled with thousands to where soccer moms and dads gather with their lattes to the water cooler where people gather to discuss this charismatic mixed-race man who would be president.

Some call him Black, but he, like Tiger Woods, has said in the past that it is a statement that short changes his entire heritage—after all, it was his mother, a White woman from Kansas, and her parents who raised him. His Kenyan father, however, fills his imagination and psyche as is evident in his memoir *Dreams from My Father,* described by Kamiya as follows: "the story of Obama's personal evolution and parochialism to a universal humanism. It's also the story of how a man blessed with a powerful analytical mind developed emotional intelligence along the way. Obama's tortured interior quest forced him to stare down all the demons in his, and America's, racial closet."[3]

Civil rights activist Al Sharpton weighed in:

> "A black candidate doesn't want to look like he's only a black candidate," the Rev. Al Sharpton, who ran for president in 2004, said in an interview about Mr. Obama. If he over identifies with Sharpton, he looks like he's only a black candidate. A White candidate reaches out to a Sharpton and looks like they have the ability to reach out. It looks like they're presidential. That's the dichotomy.[4]

Yet, for all intents and purposes Obama does look like your typical African American, which of course incorporates with its broad brush those who used to be called mulatto and a countless number of similar monikers. Biracial, bicultural, and proud of it, Obama has become a unifying force who seeks to look beyond race, seeing it as an old and divisive concept, looking toward the hope that change of thinking and new ways of being can bring to the United States. Obama was one of few recent presidential candidates to steer the conversation of race into a positive and new direction that is unifying rather than divisive, and for that he is greatly appreciated and applauded in the mixed-race, as well as broader, community.

Walking the Color Tightrope

In closing on Obama and the executive branch of government, for the moment at least, I leave you with another quote by yet another journalist, Janny Scott:

NATIVE AMERICAN VICE PRESIDENT CHARLES CURTIS

At this point, Barack Obama is leading in the polls and has a good chance of becoming one of our biracial, African American presidents, the first popularly accepted as such, though others are rumored to have been of multiracial heritage, including Abraham Lincoln, who is thought to be of Melungeon heritage by some through his mother's bloodline. The recognized multiracial vice president, according to the Mixed Heritage Center, is Charles Curtis, who lived from January 24, 1860, to February 8, 1936. His mother, Ellen Pappan Curtis, was one-fourth Kaw, one-fourth Osage, and one-fourth Pottawatomie, as well as one-fourth French. Vice President Curtis spent part of his childhood on a Kaw reservation and is the first and only person with acknowledged non-European (mixed) ancestry to reach either of the two highest offices in the U.S. government's executive branch.[a]

[a] Louie Gong, Mixellaneous. Mixed People You Didn't Know Were Mixed (blog), http://www.mixedheritagecenter.org/index.php?option=com_content&task=view&id+1445&Itemid=29 (accessed July 13, 2008).

Much of Mr. Obama's success as a politician has come from walking a fine line—as an independent Democrat and a progressive in a state dominated by the party organization and the political machine, and as a biracial American whose political ambitions require that he appeal to whites while still satisfying the hopes and expectations of blacks.

Like others of his generation, he is a member of a new class of politicians. Too young to have experienced segregation, he has thrived in white institutions. His style is more conciliatory than confrontational, more technocrat that preacher. Compared with many older politicians, he tends to speak about race indirectly or implicitly, when he speaks about it at all.[5]

From White to Colored: The Story of Sandra Laing

While Barack Obama knew his parents were interracial from the start, Sandra Laing did not have that very worthy bit of information with which to work. Born and raised, for a while at least, as a White Afrikaner girl, Sandra lived a fairly comfortable middle-class life. Her parents, two shopkeepers, were a part of the apartheid-supporting national political party, which held Blacks and people of color as unequal citizens for centuries.

Born at a hospital for Whites only in Amersfoort, a village of sheep farmers about 50 miles from Brereton Park, her parents lived in Balmoral, an even tinier *dorp* (village) than Amersfoort.[6] Her birth certificate records the date she was born as November 26, 1955; her Christian name was recorded as Susanna Magrietha (named for her mother); her sex, female; and her color, *blanke* (White). Like many children of color, she started very pale with hair indistinguishable from that of a Caucasian.

As Sandra grew, however, it became apparent that she came from a very complex gene pool. Her skin darkened to a honey brown, and her hair curled tightly, so she wore a short 'fro. Under apartheid, especially, it was critical to be categorized racially since most of the normal aspects of everyday life were controlled and prescribed by race. Upon seeing Sandra's physical "developments," the Director of the Census officially changed her classification from White to "colored." She had brothers, but they remained categorized as White.

Now, there was a huge wrench thrown into her family life. She could no longer legally enter the same restaurants, theaters, swimming pools, or clinics as her parents. Nor could she share the same bus seat, park bench, or even cemetery grounds when she passed away. According to the letter of the law, she could no longer even live with her White family, unless she was their servant, nor could she attend the only school she had ever known.[7]

Blacks were to live in the evenings in what were called "townships" or "native locations"; by day they served the Whites as cooks, housecleaners, launderers, and gardeners—out of sight of the Piet Relief where Sandra lived.[8] Even with the color line drawn taut, Sandra's three best friends were Swazi from the Black township of Driefontein.[9]

At the tender age of 6, Sandra began to be confronted by others ill-at-ease with her appearance and place in her family. By 10, after suffering humiliation and intense racism in her neighborhood and at school from both classmates as well as the administration, she was kicked out of school. Her father, Abraham Laings, who passed DNA paternity tests as her birth father, fought hard legally to keep her in school and to keep her rightful place as a White child through the court systems.

Quite the newsmaker, the young Sandra has two television documentaries chronicling her life, and numerous magazine articles explained the genetic means that could account for her African-descended appearance though she was born into a White family. Antiapartheid activists cite her case as a grisly reminder of the randomness, cruelty, and insanity of racial classifications in general.[10]

> "Apparently, in South Africa just like everywhere else, Blacks and Whites have been crossing the invisible color line and creating children for nearly three hundred years," says Anco, an Afrikaner who was raised in Swaziland. "We're all mixed blood here, so what does it matter?"[11] he concludes.

The South African geneticist J. A. Hesse, who published in the early 1970s, stated after close study of colonial marriage and birth records that

NOTES FROM J. A. HEESE

The flaw in the blood of the half-caste destroys the peace of community by revisiting its sins upon it. Mixed blood is a harbinger of doom to someone who thinks like Sara Gertrude Millin.

—*J. M. Coetzee*

The coloured race is untidiness in God's earth—a mixture of degenerate brown peoples, rotten with sickness—an affront against nature.

—Sara Gertrude Millin, *God's Stepchildren.* (London: Constable, 1924, quoted in J. M. Coetzee, "Blood, Taint, Flaw, Degeneration: The Case of Sarah Gertrude Millin," *English Studies in Africa* 23, no 1 (1980: 41–58.)

about 8 percent of the genes of the modern Afrikaner are non-White. This earned him death threats to be sure. More recent DNA studies of the Afrikaner community put the number slightly higher at 11 percent, based on the presence of mutations and markers specific to Black Africans. This is due to the fact that similarly to colonial America, the number of White men far exceeded that of White women. European farmers had sexual unions with slaves and the Khoi and San (bush people), sometimes marrying the Khoi and San women. Some of the children looked and lived as Whites (which could explain Sandra's situation), but mainly they were considered *kleurling* (colored).[12]

The same tired theories circulated in South Africa as in the United States regarding the innate inferiority of mixed-raced people. Husband-and-wife team Harold B. Fantham, a zoologist, and Annie Porter, a parasitologist, asserted that "colored" people, as a hybrid race, were naturally unstable and less intelligent than Whites. The couple claimed their research proved that racial mixture led to physical and mental abnormalities. Unfortunately, Sandra's parent's ascribed to the couple's racist views even when it came to their own flesh and blood.

FIRST TRAUMA, THEN TRAVERSING THE RACIAL BARRIER

Sometimes I wonder how things might have been, what life might have been like, if I was born white. Mostly I try just to forget the past . . . I'm much happier with black people. I am. I was very shy with white people. Even today, I still think white people don't like black people because of the way they treated me.

—Sandra Laing[13]

Sandra's parents put their daughter's appearance down to an unspecified interracial union way back in her family history, but the neighbors were sure her mother had committed adultery, which shamed the family. This came as a shock to the parents. According to Sannie Laing, Sandra's mother, "I was over the moon when my daughter was born. We were members of the South Africa's Nationalist Party and Dutch Reformed Church. As such, we lived for our country, church and family." Still, they urged their daughter, "don't listen," and "pay no attention." Gradually Sandra shut down, as instructed, relinquishing her assessments of who she was and retreating as traumatized children do, eventually reduced to bedwetting and social withdrawal.[14]

Sandra ended up running away from home, eloping at 16 with Petrus Zwane, a Zulu speaker, and becoming a teenage mother in a very abusive relationship. Says Sandra: "My father was furious because I married a black man. He threatened to shoot first me then himself if I ever put my foot over his threshold again."[15]

It was a step into another world, from ruling-caste privilege, enjoyed by Whites only, to the oppression and poverty of the townships. From apartheid there was no escape: Sandra could not keep her two children unless she was reclassified as "colored," but her father refused to consent.[16]

Eventually, she remarried and opened her own shop, following in the footsteps of her parents. Today, she has five children and many grandchildren, as well as the scars from her very peculiar upbringing. There have been many feature stories about Sandra Laing, as I mentioned, and a film is planned by Miramax.

REVELATIONS OF MY OWN

What I have endured because of my color has been intense but is incomparable to what Sandra Laing went through. However, the very act of writing this book, from a personal perspective, has meant I have had revelations of my own. The writing has been a much longer, drawn-out process than planned, taking about triple the time to pen than planned, largely due to the twists and turns as a result of personal discoveries I was met with around each corner and back alley of research.

During this lengthy gestation period, I have had visions of my childhood, teenage years, and adult life. As a young child, I was race shielded: content, colorless. As I grew, I had new names hurled at me: yellow, from the people I considered my own; nigger, from self-identified Whites mostly. There were the background jeers as well—Nigger-Rican, or the more intimately offensive . . . "but you're not like them," or "no offense," the buffer statement I'd often hear before the onslaught of racial slurs.

ON BEING: NIGGER-RICAN OR *ZAMBO*

I wonder whose racial and cultural background will match my own. I get silence for an answer. For those of us who fall between the cracks being "black," being "white," being "Chinese," being "Latino" is complicated.

—Claudine Chiawei O'Hearn[17]

I want to dwell for the moment on the pejorative *Nigger-Rican,* because even my father playfully gave me this nickname. Before my series of DNA tests, I identified almost solely as African American and Black, though when I had anyone express sincere interest in my ethnicity, I would also go into the details that I was part European and part Native American as well. My intriguing recognition recently is that genetically and ancestrally, I could also identify as Latino or Hispanic, even though I don't speak Spanish and it was not a part of the ethos of my household growing up.

Some but not all of my Spanish heritage undoubtedly comes from my paternal grandfather. This puts me in a space where I can better appreciate the transracial adoptive experience for some—not knowing the entirety of whom I am ethnically or culturally due to lack of information. I cling instead to what is known of my heritage and my DNA test results, yet I live with the certainty that there is much more to be discovered about my true ancestry.

I am at a curious crossroads with all of this. I will always be of clear African descent. This is something that brings pride as it honors my African ancestors, yet it isn't the entire story, not even in my phenotype.

Today, I see that the terms *Latina* and *Hispanic* are open and inclusive enough to include someone like me—perhaps you recognize these aspects in your ancestry as you're reading and thinking? Sometimes, it takes a moment. Latinas and Hispanics include Spanish heritage and Native American background—my great, great, great grandmother—a Ware, was Native American, seemingly a mixture of Cherokee and Virginia's First Nations, Pamunkey or perhaps Rappahannock.

ATLANTIC CREOLES

My Hunt/Hurst ancestry was traced by genealogist and historian extraordinaire Paul Heinegg to Faithy Hurst, a White woman born in 1757. Faithy gave birth to and immediately manumitted a son of mixed-race (European and African) descent.[18] Not much is known in my family about Faithy, apart from her genealogy; however, it is safe to say that her descendants as listed in Heinegg's book, *Free African Americans of North Carolina, Virginia and South Carolina from the Colonial Period to About 1820,* as some of the older free people of color inhabitants of the Virginia Colony, were what were considered Atlantic Creoles.

Atlantic Creoles were members of the first generation in the Chesapeake Colony. Through the first 50 years of settlement, lines were less rigid than today between Black and White workers; often both were indentured servants, and slaves were not as segregated as they were later.[19] Many relationships developed between White women and Black men. According to Heinegg:

> Many relationships grew between white women and black men. The new generation of creoles were the children of freed slaves and indentured servants of European, West African, and Native American ancestry (and not just North American, but also Caribbean, Central and South American Indian) who were born in the colonies. When the mothers were white, as was often the case, the children were considered free. These families with white mothers and African or African American fathers were the origins of most of the free people of color during the colonial period, and they were called Atlantic Creoles.[20]

Some Atlantic Creoles were what we would today call Latino/Latina, with surnames such as Chavez, Rodriguez, and Francisco. Many of them were in interracial marriages with their English and Irish neighbors, adopting their surnames; some became property owners and farmers who owned slaves themselves. The families were well-established, with numerous descendants by the time of the American Revolution.

AFRO-SPANISH

Outside of South, East, North, and West African, respectively, my heritage is what is called Afro-Spanish, and this was one of my highest world-population matches on the test I took through DNA Tribes. I am exploring my Spanish-ness, what people rudely called "Nigger Rican," through culture, dance, art, and food. I am considering studying the Spanish language or Portuguese, which I also have as a strong secondary ethnicity. Meanwhile, I feel blessed to have the opportunity to consider myself descended from the Atlantic Creoles, a *Zambo, Mestizo,* or *Meste,* yet knowing an honoring the fact that I am African American and embracing all that each term means, and can mean, to my life and ways of being in the world with

NAMING MIXED RACE IN SPAIN AND ITS COLONIES

African + Spaniard + Spaniard + Amerindian + African

=	=	=	=
Mulatto	Criollo	Mestizo	Zambo

groups of people I had considered "other." This is a meaningful part of my life's journey.

Zambos

As I've mentioned and illustrated, there are slews of names for people of color. *Zambo* is a Spanish term (the Portuguese language term is *Cafuso*) that was used during the Spanish Empire and continues to be used today to identify individuals in Hispanic America who are of mixed African and Amerindian ancestry. The word, originating in the Romance languages, has the feminine form *Zamba.* Though this word is seldom used in English, there are plenty of North American *Zambos* including the singers Tina Turner (African-Amerindian) and Mariah Carey (European/Irish, Afro-Venezuelan descent), news anchor/journalist Soledad O'Brien (Australian/Irish and Afro-Cuban), and guitarist Jimi Hendrix (African-Amerindian).

In Latin America, *Zambos* represent small minorities in the northwestern South American countries of Columbia, Venezuela, and Ecuador. A small but noticeable number of them live in the major coastal cities of Ecuador—results of the unions of Amerindian women and Afro-Ecuadorian men. These populations of mixed Amerindian and African ancestry are generally marginalized and discriminated against, though some individuals have very high profiles, for example, the very proud, Venezuelan President Hugo Chávez, who has made favorable comments about being of African and Amerindian descent publicly.

Zambos[21] were initially the offspring of escaping shipwrecked slaves, as well as plantation slave escapees who ventured into various Central American, South American, and Caribbean forests, seeking refuge and freedom in remote Amerindian communities. In Latin America, these primarily African settlements of runaways or Maroons were called *quilombos.* The most famous of all *quilombos* are the legendary Palmares of Brazil,

ENGLAND TODAY

In 2000, the *Sunday Times,* a British publication, reported that Britain has the highest rate of interracial relationships in the world. They are speaking of the mix of Anglo-British; Caribbean, African, and Asian, such as Leona Lewis, winner of the American-Idol in Britain. Leona is a British singing sensation who is of a very complex blend: Afro-Caribbean Guyanese from her father's side and Welsh from her mother's side of the family.

which at its height had a population of over 30,000 people. On the Island of Hispaniola, for example, present-day Haiti and the Dominican Republic, escaped enslaved people encountered the few remaining *Tainos* on the island and mixed with them. Today these Afro-Amerindians, or *Zambos,* make up a small percentage of the populations of both Haiti and the Dominican Republic.[22]

ZAMBO, HAPA, AND BLASIAN: SUPERMODEL TYSON BECKFORD

We aren't use to thinking of the hard times of a supermodel; however, for some mixed-raced models there are considerable trials and tribulations before and even while famous. Take the example of Tyson Beckford. He is Zambo, being Jamaican and Panamanian, and he is also Blasian (Black-Asian) and what used to be referred to as Hapa[23] since his mother is Chinese American. Despite his contented looks, he has not had an easy road. He was bathed in derogatory names and generally made fun of largely because of his clearly defined African and Asian blended appearance while growing up in both Jamaica and New York.

Race has been at the forefront of his mind from that time onward. He turned down a prestigious catwalk position in Milan because no other men of African descent were offered a similar opportunity. In 1995, he was named VH1's "Model of the Year." Recently, he has been cohost and judge of *Make Me a Supermodel.* His mellow and accepting, nurturing personality comes through the camera.

Beckford is proud and at ease with his ancestry, which is the foundation of the looks that have won him worldwide acclaim as a supermodel, beginning as a top Ralph Lauren model. It is notable that Ralph Lauren seeks an "all-American" look. Tyson Beckford's obvious mixed-race appearance puts him squarely into the category of "all-American," as a representative of the *Zambo* and Blasians that are a part of America's melting pot. Rather than resting on his laurels, Tyson relishes his role as a multiracial trailblazer and has made it his mission to help other men of color, in particular, break into the modeling world.

ENTER THE CABLINASIAN: TIGER WOODS

To thicken the melting pot further, enter someone called Tiger Woods, arguably one of the greatest contemporary golfers in the world. Wood went through his early career under the label "Black," but it was uncomfortable because for him it did not ring true and was "given" instead of retrieved by him as a way of self-identification. Creative as well as extremely athletic, Woods coined his own term to describe his complex ethnicity, which is, according to him, one-quarter Thai, one-quarter Chinese, one-eighth Native American, one-eighth White, and one-eighth African descended. He calls himself Cablanasian (ca: Caucasian; bl: Black; an: American Native and Asian).

According to Ramona Douglass, biracial president of the AMEA on speaking about Tiger Woods:

"He has made it clear he has no reason to deny his mother," Douglass said. "Whether he wants to or not, he is sort of becoming the poster person for multiracial identity."[24]

Tiger Woods, by virtue of the one-drop rule would be seen as African American because of his appearance and that of his father. Until recently that is how he was referred to in the media. But Woods quickly began correcting reporters, telling them he would be denying his mother by allowing media to describe him only as Black. In 1995 before playing his first U.S. Open, Woods went further and issued a press release about his racial background. "The various media have portrayed me as an African-American sometimes Asian," he said in the short statement. "In fact, I am both . . . truthfully, I feel very fortunate and equally proud to be both African-American and Asian."

Wood's celebrity status has gained him tremendous popularity in Thailand. In fact, just as many African Americans say Woods is Black because he looks Black, many Thai Americans say Woods is Thai because his facial features reflect the people of Thailand. Edward Lin, a restaurateur and golf ball manufacturing company owner, said he immediately identified with Woods after reading about him in a Thai magazine. "He has Thai blood. We recognize that part of him," said Lin, who lives in Northbrook, Illinois. "Everyone is proud of that. It is something to relate to."[25]

IT'S MY CHOICE: IN VOICE OF ACTRESS HALLE BERRY

While some chose to own and bring social change through identifying as multiracial, mixed race, or even Cablinasian, there are other high-profile people who chose a single identity, such as Halle Berry. According to Berry:

I was raised by my white mother and every day of my life, I have always been aware of the fact that I am bi-racial. However, growing up I was aware that even though my mother was white, I did not look or "feel" very white myself . . . Many times my classmates did not believe me when I said my mother was white. I soon grew tired of trying to prove that I was half-black and half-white and learned not to concern myself with what others thought. I began to relate to other "all black kids" at my school more because quite simply . . . I looked more like them . . . After having many talks with my mother about the issue, she reinforced what she had always taught me. She said that even though you are half black and half white, you will be discriminated against in this country as a black person. People will

> not know when they see you that you have a white mother unless you wear a sign on your forehead. And, even if they did, so many people believe that you have an ounce of black blood in you then you are black. So, therefore, I decided to let folks categorize me however they needed to. I realized that my sense of self and my sense of self-worth was not determined by the color of my skin or what ethnic group I chose to be a part of . . . We are all members of the same race, the HUMAN RACE! . . . I have realized that being viewed as only BLACK I am in a wonderful position. I can continue to blaze a trail for black women in film and television and help open the minds of those who have been victims of the racist teachings of the past. If through my life I can help obliterate the negative images of black people and help to abolish the negative stereotypes associated with black people . . . then when I die I will know my life had real purpose.[26]

Whereas once our lives were prescribed—we were told, you are Black or you are White, Indian, yellow, colored, mulatto, Zambo . . . whatever—today we have the freedom to chose to identify with a single culture or multiple cultures. This is an important act of reclaiming. No matter what it is you chose to be, it is you who now has the opportunity to make that choice.

NOTES

1. Jason Carroll, "Behind the Scenes: Is Barack Obama Black or Biracial?" CNN's American Morning, http://www.cnn.com/2008/POLITICS/06/09/btsc.obama.race/index.html (accessed July 10, 2008).
2. Gary Kamiya, "Biracial, but Not Like Me," Salon.com, February 5, 2008, p. 2, http://www.salon.com/opinion/kamiya/2008/02/05/obama_race/print.html (accessed July 10, 2008).
3. Ibid, 1.
4. Janny Scott, "The Long Run: A Biracial Candidate Walks His Own Fine Line," December 29, 2007, http://www.nytimes.com/2007/12/29/us/politics/29obama.html?_r=1&oref+slogin&pagew (accessed July 10, 2008).
5. Ibid.
6. Judith Stone, *When She Was White: The True Story of a Family Divided by Race* (New York: Miramax Books [Hyperion], 2007), 24–25.
7. Ibid., 6.
8. Ibid., 9.
9. Ibid., 26.
10. Ibid., 14.
11. Ibid., 15.
12. Ibid., 62, 64.
13. "The Black Woman—With White Parents," Guardian Unlimited, February 17, 2003, http://www.buzzle.comeditorials/3–17–2003–37452.asp (accessed July 16, 2008).
14. Stone, *When She Was White,* 60.
15. Stone, *When She Was White,* 140.
16. "The Black Woman—With White Parents," Guardian Unlimited.
17. Claudine Chiawei O'Hearn, ed., *Half and Half* (New York: Pantheon Books, 1998), xiv.

18. Paul Heinegg, *Free African Americans of North Carolina, Virginia and South Carolina from the Colonial Period to About 1820* (Baltimore: Clearfield Co., 2007).

19. Ira Berlin, *Many Thousands Gone: The First Two Centuries of Slavery in North America* (Cambridge, MA: Belknap Press, 1998), 29–33.

20. Heinegg, *Free African Americans of North Carolina, Virginia and South Carolina from the Colonial Period to About 1820.*

21. In certain places, the word *Zambo* is a racist word used to describe individuals of African descent.

22. Ibid.

23. *Hapa* means "half" in traditional Hawaiian language; it has come to stand for people of mixed-race Asian heritage in North America.

24. Janita Poe, "Tiger Woods Spotlights Multiracial Identity; Golf Star Sparks Pride in Heritage," *Chicago Tribune,* 1997.

25. Ibid.

26. "Race Relations: Celebrities in Hollywood Today," http://racerelations.about.com/od/celebritiesandrace/hollywoodtoday.htm?p=1 (accessed July 16, 2008).

CHAPTER 10

The State of the Mixed Union: What's Happening in the Government, on Campus, on the Internet, and in the News

> "Almighty God created the races, white, black, yellow, Malay, and red and placed them on separate continents, and but for the interference with his arrangement there would be no cause for such marriages. The fact that he separated the races shows that he did not intend the races to mix."
>
> *Judge Bazile, Caroline County, Virginia, 1965*

SOLEDAD O'BRIEN AND THE LOVING DECISION

It might surprise you to hear that antimiscegenation laws affect even public personalities you know today, but that is sadly the case. Living in contemporary times it is hard to imagine having to live by laws that prevent you from marrying the person you love, but until not long ago, that was exactly the case.

The parents of CNN's Special Units investigator and journalist, and anchor of the year-long special "Black in America," Soledad O'Brien, could not get legally married where they lived, which was the state of Maryland, what many consider the border state of the South. O'Brien's parents—her mother of Afro-Cuban descent, and her father of Australian-Irish descent—found themselves squarely netted in the antimiscegenation legislation as a young couple.

O'Brien's full name is Maria de la Soledad Teresa O'Brien, which means in Spanish, the "Blessed Virgin Mary of Soledad." She is not a strong Spanish speaker, though people expect it of her, another prejudice to which Afro-Latinas are sometimes subjected. Soledad identifies as Hispanic (Latina) and Black. While her parents were able to triumph by simply moving their wedding plans to Washington, D.C., and then having all of her siblings and herself attend Harvard University, the story of her parents still demonstrates the importance of protective civil rights laws while highlighting the need for Loving Day.

What's Happening Around June 12?

Loving Day is an education community observation. The name is derived from *Loving v. Virginia (1967)*, the landmark Supreme Court decision that legalized interracial marriage in the United States. Loving Day is a special day set aside to commemorate the anniversary of the Loving decision every year on or around June 12.

Loving Goals

According to Lovingday.org, the goals of the holiday are as follows:

1. Create a common connection between multicultural communities, groups, and individuals.
2. Foster multicultural awareness, understanding, acceptance, and identity.
3. Fight prejudice by educating the public about the history of interracial relationships.
4. Set aside a space for the tradition of Loving Day celebrations as a means to achieve these goals.

Loving Day: Suggested Activities

Pot luck, barbeque, or dinner party—make a toast or spend some time with someone you love. It is most important to make Loving Day your own and to spread the word to others in the community who might not know about it.

GENERATION MIX (HTTP://WWW.GENERATIONMIX.ORG)

Started in 2005 and run by enthusiastic members of the post–Loving decision, (a new generation called "mixed raced baby boomers," who are also a part of generations X and Y), several advocacy groups have arisen to build awareness about the issues faced by mixed-race people. The MAVIN Foundation is one such group. MAVIN is behind the "Generation Mix National Awareness Tour." The tour is led by five mixed-race youth, who travel 8,000 miles across 17 cities, in a 26-foot RV driving from Seattle to Boston with the purpose of spreading awareness and education about multiracial issues and the resources of the foundation.[1]

Despite the fact that multiracial Americans constitute a rapidly growing population, few schools and social service agencies are dedicated to multiracial youths. Generation Mix Tour seeks to expose the dangers of being underserved as well as pointing out useful resources. The founder of the group criticized current employment, education, and other institutions for failing to transform with the times. "Too often we are confronted with having to check just one box, making us feel like we don't exists," says Kelley.[2] Complying with this demand not only forces people to choose one race over another, he says, it also forces the resignation of multiracial people to statistical insignificance. This can lead to very serious issues—for one thing, multiracial individuals encounter different problems of health care than mono-racial people. In particular, it is more difficult to find matches for bone marrow transplants among multiracial people, increasing the threat of diseases like leukemia. Raising awareness about such problems leads to increased availability of viable local resources with which to tackle such issues.

Generation Mix tackles the issue of transracial adoption as well. According to Kelly:

> When children of color are placed with white parents, questions arise that go far beyond differences in complexion. Exploration of one's heritage takes another dimension when one's parents belong to a different ethnicity.[3]

Kelly says the MAVIN Foundation is working to bring light to such issues of identity, but he emphasizes that this can only be accomplished with the help of parents, teachers, and social workers who must become more aware of mixed-race issues.

The coast-to-coast experience is

> About how to identify ways we can create spaces for mixed heritage people within existing communities." It is a movement to recognize and honor ways people self-identify. It is not merely another attempt to increase diversity, but an experience designed to expand the dialogue on race in our country.[4]

THE GROWTH AND DISTRIBUTION OF BIRACIAL UNIONS BY THE CENSUS

According to the U.S. Census, in 2000 there were

- 1,432,908 Hispanic origin to Caucasian marriages;
- 504,119 Asian to Caucasian marriages;
- 287,576 African-descended to Caucasian marriages
- 97,822 Hispanic origin to African-descended marriages

- 40,317 Asian to Hispanic-origin marriages
- 31,271 Asian to African-descended marriages

There has been a great deal of legislation and attempted legislation to prevent interracial marriages. In 1912, for example, Congressman Seaborn Roddenberry of Georgia proposed the following constitutional amendment:

> That intermarriage between negroes or person of color and Caucasians or any other character of persons within the United States or any territory under the jurisdiction is forever prohibited; and the term 'negro or person of color' as here employed shall be held to mean any and all persons of African descent or having an trace of African or negro blood.[5]

MIXED-RACE TWINS IN THE NEWS

Over the past three years, there have been mixed-race births making the news. Why? Because they so clearly illustrate the point of being mixed race. One child is born looking almost entirely like the father; the other looks like the mother. The deal is, the mother is African descended, and the father European descended, or vice versa.

In many West African cultures, twins are sacred—harbingers of luck and a symbol of certain deities. Recently in Germany, a German African couple, Florence Addo Gerth (35, of Ghana) and Stephen Gerth (40, of Germany), gave birth to twins who defy the odds by about 1 in a million—each reflects one of their parent's entire phenotypes rather than being a mixture of the two.

Ryan, the oldest twin, has pale skin and blue eyes just like his father. Leo has chocolate brown skin, dark eyes, and hair like his mother,[6] who says:

> I imagine sitting at a playground where the other mothers will call me crazy when I tell them the boys are twins.[7]

Coincidentally, the 2008 International Congress of Genetics was being held in Berlin at the time of the Gerth twins' birth on July 17, 2008. The head of the conference, Dr. Rudi Balling, said, "the (birth) event is very unusual. But it is definitely possible, because ultimately the genes of both parents are combined."[8]

A MAVIN (ONE WHO UNDERSTANDS)

Today, mixed-race children, including those twins just born, will have many questions thrust upon them throughout their lives because of their polar opposite appearance. They will need readily available resources to navigate the elaborate social labyrinth.

Matt Kelley formed a powerhouse of an organization when he was only 19 years of age and a freshman at Connecticut's Wesleyan University. He chose the name MAVIN for the organization, which has Yiddish roots and means, "one who understands." Since its inception, it has been a remarkable organization and has provided incredible resources for young people, college students, parents, social workers, teachers, and ministers working with populations of contemporary mixed-raced individuals. Here is a brief timeline of the activities of MAVIN.

1998—MAVIN began as an eagerly anticipated magazine.

2002—Two MAVIN foundation interns conduct MAVIN's first bone marrow drive to help a biracial girl from Seattle fight against leukemia.

2003—MAVIN published *The Multiracial Child Resource Book: Living Complex Identities,* a 288-page guide to assist parents, teachers, and professionals raise happy and healthy mixed-race youths. The book is coedited by area experts Maria P. P. Root, Ph.D. and Matt Kelley. In the same year, MAVIN and the Association of Multiethnic Americans (AMEA) launched a national resource center to gather and disseminate the growing number of resources that address contemporary issues of mixed race and the transracial adoption experience. Also in 2003, MAVIN launched a pilot phase of its new project, the Community Mixed Race Action Plan (MAP), which helps communities interested in enhancing and developing favorable mixed-race relationships on a grassroots level.

2005—The national resource center goes into a beta version of the Web site and is called the new Mixed Heritage Center (MHC). This, too, is a joint project of MAVIN and AMEA. This year they launch their most ambitious project, Generation Mix, an 8,000-mile journey across America by five mixed-heritage twenty-somethings who wish to raise awareness of America's newest generation: the "mixed raced baby boomers."

2006 to the present—As the organization continues to grow, they have developed a campus awareness and compliance initiative (CACI) and "One Box Isn't Enough" effort in partnership with Bryn Mawr and Haverford Colleges to hand deliver over 3,000 comment cards to the U.S. Department of Education, urging them to provide guidance to U.S. schools to adopt "mark one or more races" formats. They have also embarked on their national awareness-building tour called Generation Mix National Awareness Tour. Readers can visit the information-laden Web site at http://www.mavin.org and join the organization to stay updated as well as to receive their newsletters and publications.

ASSOCIATION OF MULTIETHNIC AMERICANS (AMEA)

The Internet is a busy information hub for mixed-raced individuals. Wikipedia has many valuable entries on all types of mixed-raced people around the world as well as information on specific individuals and our history. Another very important organization akin to MAVIN that features a great deal of opportunity to both interact and gain understanding is AMEA.

According to AMEA's Web site at http://www.ameasite.org/about.asp, AMEA is an international association of organizations dedicated to advocacy education and collaboration on behalf the multiethnic, multiracial, and transracial adoption community. AMEA has three primary objectives:

1. Providing access to culturally competent resources by connecting service providers to clients.
2. Facilitate collaboration between organizations dedicated to multiethnic, multiracial, and transracial adoptee issues.
3. Conducting needs assessments to identify and meet unmet needs and recognize new trends.

Mostly, AMEA works at the local, grass-roots level. They organize social and cultural events, forums, and provide valuable information. AMEA has won recognition from the media and government and continues to engage at every opportunity to express its views and provide information on issues that concern our community, such as government form classifications, multiethnic/multiracial identity, multiracial parenting, health, education, transracial adoptions, and so forth. AMEA testified before Congress and has participated in the federal government's Census 2000 Advisory Committee with respect to how the mixed-race community is affected by not being acknowledged and counted accurately on government forms (see chapter 11 for contact information).

BIRACIAL FAMILY NETWORK

A nonprofit 501c(3) public benefit corporation to help eradicate prejudice and discrimination. Biracial Family Network, or BFN, serves individuals and families of diverse ethnic ancestry to improve the quality of their interracial and intercultural relationships, utilizing educational and social activities. BFN participated in the 1988 founding of AMEA, a national organization previously discussed. In 2000, BFN celebrated its twentieth anniversary in Chicago, Illinois. Membership is open to all people who have paid any membership dues and who ideologically support interracial/intercultural relationships. BFN can be found at http://www.bfnchicago.org for more information or membership opportunities.

MELUNGEON HERITAGE ASSOCIATION (MHA)

The mission of the group is stated on their Web site (http://www.melungeon.org): "to document and preserve the heritage and cultural legacy of mixed-ancestry peoples in or associated with the southern Appalachians . . . we will not restrict ourselves to honoring only this group (Melungeons) though it is our main focus. We firmly believe in the dignity of all such mixed ancestry groups of southern Appalachia and are committed to preserving this rich heritage of racial harmony and diversity." The MHA is a not-for-profit organization dedicated to preserving Melungeon history and heritage. MHA sponsors annual gatherings for the presentation of information about Melungeons. The gatherings are only one aspect of the work of MHA.

The primary area of concern is telling the story of the Melungeon people and continuing to put together its mosaic past, which has been buried for so long. MHA has the mission to document and preserve the heritage and cultural legacy of mixed-ancestry people in and around the southern Appalachian mountain regions. For more information visit the Web site or via postal mail (see chapter 11 for contact information).

MIXED HERITAGE CENTER

The Mixed Heritage Center (MHC), is a collaboration between the MAVIN Foundation and the Association of Multiethnic Americans. Its purpose is to serve as a clearinghouse of information and resources relevant to the lives of people who are multiracial, multiethnic, transracially adopted, or otherwise impacted by the intersections of race and culture. It is an organic resource that continues to grow and change with the contributions of users.

Louie Gong, Joe Sakay, and Jenee Jahn coordinate the MHC, and they can be reached at contact@mixedheritagecenter.org (the MHC Web site is located at http://www.mixedheritagecenter.org).

Mixed Chicks Film and Literary Festival

Mixed Chicks Chat is the only live weekly podcast about racially and culturally mixed America. The hosts are Fanshen Cox and Heidi Durrow, who perform LIVE each Wednesday at 5 P.M. ET and 2 P.M. PT to discuss all aspects of the mixed experience. The podcast can be found at http://www.talkshoe.com (keywords: Mixed Chicks). The call-in number for the day of the show only is 724-444-7444.

Mixed Chicks Chat sponsors the Mixed Roots Film & Literary Festival held on or near Loving Day. The festival brings together film and book lovers, innovative artists, and families interested in the mixed racial and cultural experience. More information is available from the Heart Productions Inc., 1455 Mandalay Beach, Oxnard, California 93035, attention: Mixed Roots Film and Literary Festival. Also visit http://www.mixed chickschat.com.

NATIRAH HERITAGE SOCIETY (NA-TEE-RAH)

On the Internet, a new group has arisen that updates the notion of Mulatto Nation—it is called Natirah Heritage Council, or NHC. At times we speak about America's melting pot as something that gradually came to be.

My contention in this book is that we are indeed a casserole that was laid together and set to cook from the nation's inception. This theory is supported by the NHC—the organization of the tan American community.

According to the Natirah Web site http://members.aol.com/Natirah/H74MX.TXT.htm.:

> The color tan was chosen as a group characteristic because it is a natural variant and its relationship to traditional standards usually to classify racial groups. Tan identity signals a return to the native hybrids triracial concept of hybridity also embraces genetic diversity and allelic destiny (natural selection).

Tan clearly reflects the native metis' physical characteristics and symbolizes a range of tastes, predilections and sympathies, associated with American hybrids of color over 200 years. It is an organization designed for restoring Mulatto group identity under the tan American rubric.

THE REDBONE HERITAGE FOUNDATION (RHF)

The purpose of The Redbone Heritage Foundation is to encourage research into the origins, history, culture, and ethnicity of people known as Redbones. Members are encouraged to conduct such research in a scientific and scholarly manner, without prejudice or predetermined conclusions. Material pertaining to the Redbones and related groups, will be preserved, published, and made available to other researchers through the organization. The Redbone Heritage Foundation is a not-for-profit organization chartered in the state of Louisiana.

Contact Information for RHF

Stacy R. Webb, President, Treasurer, and Webmaster
1341 Grapevine Rd., Crofton, Kentucky 42217, Phone: 270-985-8568
e-mail: Parrotsgrl@aol.com

SWIRL

This is a proactive, national, multiethnic organization that challenges society's notions of race through community building, education, and activism.

Swirl's Core Values

1. The persistence of racism and discrimination necessitates a movement of people with a desire for change.
2. It is vital for individuals with mixed-race identities to create space to continue challenging traditional notions of race with the goal of creating a more inclusive and fair society.
3. An all-inclusive society should embrace all individuals, affording them the dignity and autonomy to identify themselves in the ways they desire.

4. Identity is not fixed but developed and decided through the influence of history, context and personal experience.
5. While race does not exist biologically, its consequences are real. Swirl is committed to working for positive change.
6. Discovery and education are the two first steps towards creating the change desired in society.
7. Creating dialogue around race and identity among diverse communities is important.
8. Understanding the significance of going beyond the specific concerns of the mixed community to take collective action in challenging discrimination on a larger scale (from Swirl's Web site http://www.swirlinc.org/ (accessed October 15, 2008).

According to Swirl Director and Founder Jean Lau:

In 2000, many of us found ourselves having to explain the idea of mixed identity to others. From strangers to our own families, we have had to answer the questions of people who didn't believe or couldn't fathom that we could be "more than one thing" at the same time. We have been asked to choose time and time again — and that's when we were actually presented with the choice — many times, people have chosen for us. Swirl was created in order to challenge the idea that identity is simple — something that can be discussed in black and white terms. I wanted to create a space where people could find community amongst others who thought about ethnicity and identity in more open-minded ways. I wanted Swirl to become a community of children and adults, young and old, interracial couples and families to share experiences, support one another, and to learn together in order to create change and move us from the borders to a space that was inclusive of all. (from Swirl's Web site http://www.swirlinc.org/ (accessed October 15, 2008)

There are many ways to become involved with Swirl, including starting your own chapter in your city (see the Web site for information on how to go about doing this). Swirl has the following participatory groups set up on the Internet:

- **Yahoo group** at: http://groups.yahoo.com/group/SWIRLinc
- **Facebook** space at: http://www.facebook.com/group.php?gid=23334 868624
- **MySpace** account at: http://www.myspace.com/332244826

Further Contact:

Swirl has chapters in the San Francisco Bay area, Boston, Washington, D.C., Arizona, Atlanta, Miami, and New York City. For more information, visit http://www.swirlinc.org.

UNPLEASANT CHILDHOOD MEMORIES: IN LIVING COLOR

According to Caribbean chanteuse Rihanna, who was born in Saint Michael, Barbados:

It made me angry; it made me want to fight in my younger years. Having lighter skin wasn't a problem in my household, but it was when I went to school—which really confused me at first. For the first six years of school, I would go home traumatized. The harassment continued to my very last day of elementary school.[9]

The Topaz Club

It's not everyday that a celebrity like Rhiannon steps forward to speak out against something as ingrained yet seldom discussed as colorism, but that is precisely what she did as cover girl during an *InStyle* magazine interview. Women and girls such as Rhiannon who suffer the ill will of colorism, that is, being disliked for their skin complexion, will find solace in groups such as The Topaz Club since it is dedicated to mixed-race, African-descended females of all ethnicities.

Founded in January 2004, the Topaz Club, known as TTC, is an Internet-based social support sisterhood for biracial and multiracial women and girls who are of African American descent in combination with other heritages.

TTC Goals

1. To build a social, professional and support network for TTC membership.
2. To provide a forum to discuss issues that affect multiracial women and girls.
3. Serving as an educational portal to help us become more educated about diverse heritages.
4. Primarily TTC seeks to address the needs and interests of the biracial and multiracial female who is part black racially, especially since there are unique challenges to be faced in identity, politics family and friendly relationships within the black community (from the Topaz Club's Web site http://www.thetopaz club.com (accessed October 24, 2008).

Meetings

Online

General discussions about issues relevant to TTC focus take place between members at the online community space through http://www.thetopazclub.com.

In Person

Occasional sisterhood brunches/dinners and social outings in cities where TTC has branches.

More information follows in the final chapter, which comes next.

NOTES

1. Suemedha Sood, "Generation Mix" Wire Tap, (posted on January 28, 2005; printed on July 13, 2008), http://www.wiretapmag.org/21117/ (accessed October 15, 2008).

2. Ibid.

3. Ibid.

4. Ibid.

5. Congressional Record, 62nd Congress, 3rd session, December 11, 1912. vol. 49, p. 502.

6. "Black and White Twins for Ghanaian-German Couple," Modern Ghana News, http://www.modernghana.com/news/174934/1/black-and-white-twins-for-ghanaian-german-couple.html (accessed October 15, 2008).

7. "Black and White Twins Born to German Mixed-Race Couple, Berlin," RIA Novosti, World, http://en.rian.ru/world/20080717/114249359.html (accessed July 18, 2008).

8. "Black and White Twins for Ghanaian-German Couple," Modern Ghana News, http://www.modernghana.com/news/174934/1/black-and-white-twins-for-ghanaian-german-couple.html (accessed October 15, 2008).

9. "August Cover Girl Story," *InStyle*, August 2008.

CHAPTER 11

A Tool Box for Change: News to Use

At the end of the twentieth century, major changes that have recently occurred in American society offer hope for the realization of better race relations in the twenty-first century. These include the dynamic force of generational replacement, the shifting of the demographic landscape, the growth of a strong Black middle class, the enlistment of large numbers of racial minorities in the U.S. military, and the gradual erosion of racial boundaries resulting from increasing rates of interracial marriages and transracial adoptions. These changes make it difficult to maintain the status quo in relation to race.

Generational replacement and demographic changes weaken the foundations on which race is socially constructed, as each successive generation of Americans becomes more tolerant and supportive of racial integration and equality. Greater access to education, increased interaction among individuals from different racial backgrounds, and society's growing intolerance of racist attitudes and behaviors consolidate this trend. The influx of immigrants also helps weaken racial boundaries by complicating the concept of race and racial categorization.[a]

---

[a] Richard J. Payne, *Getting Beyond Race: The Changing American Culture* (Boulder, CO: Westview Press, 1998), 193.

There is so much ignorance, stereotyping, and shame preventing us from understanding who we really are and how we are related to various groups. The Human Genome Project has beautifully documented the genetic commonalities that exist among all humans, yet many laypeople have not yet integrated this information into their consciousness. It is my hope as a healer that this chapter will be a gift, designed to demonstrate clearly and concisely the venerable history of triracial and biracial mixes in the United States from the seventeenth century to the present.

This book concludes with a practical application. Readers are equipped with the necessary tools to track their personal relationship to biracial and triracial cultures of North America. Organizations are listed that offer community, support, sharing, and information. This is my gift to readers and to my immediate family—I am married to an Englishman, and our children are as mixed as I am. Mixed-raced children feel especially burdened since their ultimate goal as they move toward adulthood is to define their sense of self in relation to others.

The challenge is to accept a multicultural background as a blessing, recognizing that it is a reality for many people, not a social construct like race. Understanding the history of racial mixing and blended cultures allows this identity to be contextualized along with other cultural backgrounds. Ultimately, hybrid ethnicity is normal, especially with its lengthy history and the large numbers of members, not an oddity, shameful secret, or curse.

Race has caused an enormous rift in our society. Enjoying the connections implicit in being human is assisted by understanding the complexity of our multiracial heritage. By understanding our connections, perhaps the mistrust and dislike of "other" can evolve and as a nation, we can be healed. *Light, Bright, and Damned Near White* is for America, for the triracial and biracial community, and most of all it is written for the mental health and well-being of our children. This is a tool for parents, families, friends, and the large body of professionals involved with shaping the outlook of the upcoming generations to move forward.

Table 11.1
Tool Box for Change

Individuals	*Images/Perceptions*	*Strategies for Change*
Biracial Triracial Cross-cultural Intercultural Multicultural Interracial Transracial adoptee Cross-cultural adoptee Adoptee Curious	I am alone. I do not belong to any group. Isolation is the natural outcome for mixed children. There is no way to figure out what groups you belong to. No group would find me as a member. My background is too complicated. My origins are obscured by the past; I can never change this fact.	**Discover: Ancestry and Genealogy** There are numerous resources for tracing genealogy; it has become a contemporary passion. Online there are many quick and relatively easy ways of getting started with understanding your background and ancestors including the following Web sites: • www.ancestry.com • www.genealogy.com These sites contain resources that help trace relatives, living and deceased, through surnames. There are also a wide variety of surname collectives and e-groups. **Test: DNA** DNA testing has made possible a level of understanding previously unavailable, particularly for those who have been adopted or who have scarce genealogical records. The tests have limitations, as the types of readings provided reflect genes adopted, though there are probably others that were not passed down. The other problem with the tests is that they give a picture based on all males or all females, not both; for example, if you are female, you can trace your matrilineal line. The reason is that the Y chromosome is passed from father to son, virtually unchanged. In the female reading, the mitochondrial DNA used reflects the maternal line. The tests are still valuable and a great starting point if there is no other adequate resource available. Some of these genealogically driven tests are as follows: • Family Tree DNA • DNA by Ancestry • National Geographic Genographic Project • Genetree • African Ancestry • DeCODEme

(*continued*)

Table 11.1
Tool Box for Change (*Continued*)

Individuals	*Images/Perceptions*	*Strategies for Change*
		DeCODEme is the most expensive and extensive test available on the market, as it contains information about genetic diseases as well as covering more genetic markers for ancestry than any other test.
Person with Native American along with other ancestry.	As a mixed-blood, half-breed, or whatever other derogatory term people attribute to my heritage, I could never belong to any solid group of Native American people, officially or even informally. People would laugh at me if I went to a pow-wow or other tribal event. I know I am part Indian, but I cannot prove it. Native Americans are isolationists and cultural elitists; they do not embrace outsiders.	**Information Is a Powerful Tool: Native American and Black Indian Groups** • The Bureau of Indian Affairs (BIA) still adheres to blood quantum as a way of gaining membership and affiliation with certain Native nations. • A card called Certificate of Degree of Indian Blood (CDIB) is required for entrance to most tribes. • BlackIndians.com exists as a less formal collective of people with biracial and triracial ancestry; it does not have the strict adherence to blood quantum or paperwork required by the above-mentioned associations. Full-blood, half-blood, and mixed Native Americans names are listed on a wide array of documents called rolls. These rolls were utilized for official reorganization, allotment of land, and certain privileges in the late 1800s through the 1900s. Though not definitive, the rolls are an excellent preliminary way of establishing a relationship to specific American Indian nations. Some of these lists are accessible free of charge on the Internet, while others require registration and payment of a fee. Here is a listing of a few. • **1817, Reservation Roll:** applicants for tract of land in the East; searchable by surname • **1871–1835, Emigration Roll:** permitted emigration to Arkansas by the Cherokee • **1830, Armstrong Roll:** records the Dancing Rabbit Creek treaty with the Choctaw • **1889, McKennon Roll:** records Choctaw of Mississippi, Louisiana, and Alabama • **1890, Wallace Roll:** lists Cherokee freedmen • **1889–1914, Index to Final Roll (also called the Dawes Roll):** permits tracing of Native American ancestry by surname

		• **1909, Guion Miller Roll:** deals with Eastern Cherokee • **1954, Ute Roll:** records full-blood Ute tribe of Utah
Community My parents feel a part of a single racial group, but I feel pulled in numerous directions culturally. I guess I feel all of the elements of my ancestry. I want to meet others like me, explore, communicate, question, and share.	I do not look White, Black, Indian, Asian, or Latino. There are not any people for me to relate to or fit in with. I need to get use to living in cultural isolation, but it is depressing. I do not want to be alone. I wonder where I can go for help. Maybe I should adopt a false persona, pretend to belong to an exotic culture I do not really just belong to just to fit in.	Proactive organizations, associations, and conferences, as well as magazines, now exist to enrich the multiracial, triracial, biracial, and transracial adopted communities. **Virtual Community: Building Community Online** **Blogs: Passive and Active Participation** Blogs are unique contemporary forms of Internet communication based on the concept of a daily journal. Blogs permit passive participation as a reader, while many encourage active participation by permitting written comments. To build a community that caters to your specific concerns, you should consider starting your own blog. Some active Internet blogs to use as a model or to read include the following: • **A Mixed Blog** **Multiracial Blog** www.multiracial.com/blog
I am from a mixed background. I would explore the complexity of my culture but only in a safe space.	I'm tired of feeling alone, yet I fear rejection. I have so many thoughts in my head that I feel like I am going to explode if I do not	

(continued)

Table 11.1
Tool Box for Change (*Continued*)

Individuals	*Images/Perceptions*	*Strategies for Change*
I have been adopted into a White family, but I am biracial.	talk with someone, but there is not anyone around here who would understand.	
I live in a very rural area. I live in conservative suburbs.	No one talks about this kind of stuff around here; it is best to keep these feelings inside.	
I am seeking spiritual guidance. I want to make my connections with others like me through organized religion.	I wonder if there are unique churches or faiths that support my multiracial, multicultural, intercultural, or biracial identity.	**Turn It Over to a Higher Power: Interfaith and Multiracial Spirituality** Church and temples afford a wonderful opportunity for building community and support. The following denominations were either founded on interfaith, intercultural, and multicultural perspectives or support or encourage them: **Baha'i**—one of the world's youngest and steadily growing religions. The message of the leader, Baha' Allah, is that divisions of race, class, creed, and nation need to be broken down and done away with. Baha'is believe humanity is one single race. There are 5 million adherents across the globe, including 2,100 ethnic, racial, and tribal groups. **Unitarian**—a noncreedal faith inspired by Judeo-Christianity and open to all. **Buddhism**—many Westerners are finding answers to combat racism through Buddhism because it has an emphasis on the interior (spiritual side) rather than outside appearances and material possessions.

<table>
<tr><td>Someone who likes helping others:
Advocate
Organizer
Leader
Mentor
Motivator
Author
Speaker</td><td>I have talked things out, read a lot, and even attended conferences; now I'm ready to act as a mentor and advocate for those from my background.</td><td>Get Involved: Join and Participate in Multiethnic Organizations
• Association of Multiethnic Americans (AMEA)
P.O. Box 341304, Los Angeles, California 90034-1304. According to their Web site (www.ameasite.org), AMEA seeks to educate and advocate on behalf of multiethnic individuals and families while helping eradicate discrimination against them. AMEA provides valuable health information through their bone marrow database resources.
• MAVIN Foundation
600 First Ave. Suite 600 Seattle, Washington 98104. This foundation has a magazine and local support group; hosts a national conference on the Mixed Race Experience; provides information on bone marrow transfer sources for mixed-race people; and is beginning a scholarship, internship, and international training program.
• Melungeon Heritage Association
P.O. Box, 4020, Wise, Virginia 24293. Reading list for educators, parents, and practitioners available on this triracial culture.
• American Society of Folklore
Learn about the diverse populations in the United and the world, so that your vision will not be limited to Black and White. This group encourages participation, has an annual conference, and produces an academic quarterly, Journal of American Folklore. Contact: AFS Executive Director, Timothy Lloyd, Mershon Center, Ohio State University, 1501 Neil Ave., Columbus, Ohio 43201-2602 (e-mail Lloyd.100@osu.edu).</td></tr>
<tr><td>A non-Australian person, nonaboriginal person
Healer
Attorney
Civil rights activist</td><td>It is sad about what happened to the Australian Aborigines and Torres Strait Islanders, but I live too far away to do anything to help.</td><td>Journey of Healing project, Council for Aboriginal Reconciliation, www.reconciliation.org.au</td></tr>
</table>

(*continued*)

Table 11.1
Tool Box for Change (*Continued*)

Individuals	*Images/Perceptions*	*Strategies for Change*
Practitioners/Educators Psychologist Counselor Religious leader Teacher Professor Therapist Social worker Physician Librarian Writer Public speaker Interviewer Researcher Healer	This biracial, triracial, multiracial, transadoptee stuff is too complex. I do not know enough to advise or offer an opinion, even though my client/student/confidant desires help. I should just stick to the areas of my expertise and ignore the obviously troubling issue I see. Based on what I know, I will just assign this obviously mixed-race person to the group she bears the most resemblance to.	**Read, Learn, Write: Publications** These are excellent resources, provocative and open to your articles and papers as well. • **AMEA Networking News** c/o Connie Hannah, 833 Mt. Pleasant Rd., Chesapeake, Virginia 23320. AMEA published a comprehensive multiracial child resource book. • **Identity and Development: Multiracial Heritages** by Maria P. P. Root Ph.D., Matt Kelley editor and more.
I date someone from a different culture; I want to learn what I can now about blended families and communities.	It is best to stick to your own kind. No one from a different culture would ever be romantically interested in me.	Call in or subscribe, get some advice, stay up-to-date, reach out: • **Interracial/Intercultural Pride** 2625 Alcatraz, Suite 369, Berkeley, California 94705-2702, phone: 510-923-9513. • **Interrace: The Source for Interracial Living** P.O. Box 15566, Beverly Hills, California 90209.

I want to date and meet more people of different backgrounds. I am White. I am Black. I am Native American. I am Latino. I am Asian. I am a Pacific Islander. I am a little of everything. I grew up in a racist family or community. I am open minded and ready to get over racial division and cultural animosity.	I want to reach out to people from other cultures romantically, but I am afraid that maybe some kind of racism or stereotyping exists in my subconscious. People from a different culture will automatically assume I am the enemy. Race is too big a topic to overcome or even to discuss with people from different types of ancestry. People will be suspicious of me, and I don't want to have to prove myself. I'll be viewed as a phony or a fake.	• **Interracial Voice** (No longer published, but back issues of this lively magazine are still available.) • **MAVIN** Magazine (See organizations.) • **New People: The Journal for the Human Race** P.O. Box 47490, Oak Park, Michigan 48237. • **Society for Interracial Families Newsletter** 23399 Evergreen, Suite 2222, Southfield, Michigan 48075. • **Standards—The International Journal of Multicultural Studies** E-mail standards@colorado.edu for more information on this e-journal.
I am ready to make a difference. I want to learn through doing. I thirst for knowledge.	I have worked on myself and personal situation long enough; now it is time to reach out to others.	**The Power to Change Permits Evolution** It is hard work to change ingrained patterns of recognition that lead to stereotyping, yet change is vital to healing and evolution. Following are listings of various ways that you can enhance the capacity to understand the complexity of multiracial, biracial, and multiethnic identity through research, study, and direct engagement. **Understand History: For Scholars, Students, and the General Public** • Diedre, L. Badejo, Mark Christian, *Multiracial Identity: An International Perspective,* 2000, Palgrave, Macmillan

(*continued*)

Table 11.1
Tool Box for Change (*Continued*)

Individuals	*Images/Perceptions*	*Strategies for Change*
	There probably isn't really anything out there specifically geared toward my needs and interests. We don't really have a past as mixed people, do we?	• Charles Michael Byrd *Beyond Race: The Bhagavad-Gita in Black and White,* XLIBRIS (e-book) • Ellis Cose, *Color Blind: Seeing Beyond Race in a Race Obsessed World,* 1997, Harper Collins • Kermit Hunter, *Walk Towards the Sunset* (a play) • Brent Kennedy, *The Melungeons: The Resurrection of a Proud People* 1997, Mercer University Press • Clarence Page, *Showing My Color: Impolite Essays on Race and Identity* 1997, Perennial • William Pollitzer, "The Physical and Genetics of Marginal People of the South Eastern United States," *American Anthropologist* 74, no. 3 (June 1972):719–734. • Maria Root, *The Multiracial Experience,* 1996, Sage Publications • Rita Simon, *Adoption Across Borders: Serving the Children of Transracial and Intercountry Adoptions,* 2000, Langam, Maryland: Rowman and Littlefield • Paul Spickard, *Mixed Blood: Intermarriage and Ethnic Identity in 20th Century America,* 1989, Madison: University of Wisconsin Press • Stephen Thernstrom, ed., *Harvard Encyclopedia of American Ethnic Groups,* 1980, Cambridge: Belknap Press, Harvard University Press. **Gain a Historical Perspective: Research Papers** Dr. Virginia DeMarce Mr. E. Raymond Evans Will Allen Dromgoole **Learn: For Educators and Parents (Books and Videos)** • *Multiracial Child Resource Book* by Maria Root Ph.D., Matt Kelley, editor

- *Tomorrow's Children* self-published by Dr. Francis Wardle
- **Interracial/Intercultural Pride** has a video: *Early Childhood Educators Guide "Serving Biracial and Multiethnic Children and Their Families"*
- **Center for the Study of Bi-racial Children** www.csbc.com (research facility)
- **MAVIN Foundation** and **Association of Multiethnic Americans** (www.ameasite.org) provides comprehensive reading list for educators, parents (all ages), and practitioners. (See organizations for contact information.)

Study: College-Level Courses on Multiracial Identity

- **People of Mixed Racial Descent,** annual undergraduate level course, University of California, Berkeley. Prof. Robert Allen.
- **Multiracial, Multiethnic People: The Law and Society,** law course, Golden Gate University's School of Law, San Francisco, Prof. Carlos A. Fernandez-Gray.
- **Multi-Ethnic Identity and Communities,** University of Michigan, Ann Arbor, Instructor: Karen Downing.
- **Other Than Other: The Legitimacy of a Multiracial, Multiethnic Identity,** guest lecturer at various universities, Carlos A. Fernandez-Gray.

Listen, Observe, Accept

The key to accepting the intricacy of multiracial and multiethnic identity is to listen, and accept, rather than thrust opinions based on stereotypes on others.

Index

Africa, 2, 5, 11, 34, 40, 45, 47, 51, 60, 65, 79, 81, 102, 106, 112–14, 126
African Methodist Episcopal Church (A.M.E.), 88
Afro-Ecuadorian, 117
AMEA. *See* Association of Multiethnic Americans
Amherst County, 56
Ancestors, 14, 17, 18, 19, 33, 39, 62, 91, 94, 115, 137
Ancestry, 5, 6, 7, 13–14, 17–18, 20–22, 29–31, 34, 36–37, 40, 46, 51–53, 55, 61, 63, 70, 78, 81, 84, 91–92, 94, 98, 111, 115–18, 128–29
Antebellum, 91
Appalachia, 4, 17, 36, 40, 46, 51, 54, 128–29
Association of Multiethnic Americans (AMEA), 2, 119, 127–28, 141–42, 145
Atlantic Creoles, 51, 60, 115–16
Australian Aboriginal, 103

Bal de Cordon Blue, 68
Baptist, 49, 96
Barbour County, 45, 48
Beckford, Tyson, 118
Berry, Halle, 119
Biracial, 2, 4–8, 11–12, 14, 21, 24, 27–28, 34, 47, 50, 77, 83–85, 90, 92, 103, 105, 109–11, 119, 125, 127–128, 132, 136
Black Dutch, 17, 36–39
Blackfoot, 91–92
Black Indians, 92, 98
Blackness, 14, 31, 41, 109
Blasian, 118
Brazil, 8, 20, 83, 117
Bricolage, 59–73

Cane River Negroes, 47–48, 65–66
Caucasian, 5–6, 8, 12, 38, 46, 49, 52, 59, 112, 119, 125–26
Census 2000, 2, 125, 128
Chávez, Hugo, 117
Cherokee, 16, 22, 50, 90–91, 97, 115
Chesapeake Bay, 2
Chestnut Hill People, 54, 48
Chickahominy, 56, 94–98
Chocktawhatchee River, 45, 48
Christian, 3, 45, 80, 91, 93–94, 112
Civil War, 35, 40, 48, 66, 68
Cloutierville, 47, 70
Code Noir, 71–72
Coin Coin (Marie Thereze), 65–67

Colonial: American, 21; era, 40, 72, 77, 112–13, 115–16; European, 69; precolonial, 96; Spanish, 62
Colony of Roanoke, 49, 50, 92, 94
Color line, 4, 77, 112
Colored, 5–6, 14, 16, 27, 31, 46–47, 59, 62, 64, 66, 82, 88, 90, 94, 102, 111–14, 120
Colorism, 32–33, 132
Coloured, 113. *See also* Colored
Concubinage, 68
Confederacy, 56, 66, 92, 94, 95
Contandini, 81–82
Conversos, 80
Creoles of color, 61–63, 65, 68, 70–74
Croatan, 46, 49–50
Cuba, 70

Disenfranchised, 67, 83
DNA, 5–6, 17–23, 27–28, 34, 112–13, 115–16
Dominican Republic, 3, 70, 118
Dominicker, 44, 45, 48–49
Don Antonio de Ulloa, 61–62

Ebony magazine, 98
Enslaved, 3–5, 7, 31, 45, 46, 51, 55, 61–62, 65, 67, 69, 70, 78, 80, 93, 98, 105, 118
Ethnoempathy, 85
Eugenics, 54–56

Family, 1, 14–22, 27–28, 31, 33–37, 39–40, 44–48, 51, 53, 66–67, 70, 84, 90–92, 102–5, 112, 114–15, 128, 132, 136
Folklore, 6, 33, 79
Forgotten People, 47, 56, 64–67, 70
Free people of color (FPC), 3, 48, 50, 62–64, 66, 101, 115–16
Freedman, 38–39, 62, 80, 89
Freed men, 101

Generation Mix, 124–25, 127
Gens de couleur libre, 8, 47, 56, 59, 63–68, 70–74
Gingaskin, 45, 94, 98
Gould, 43, 45–46, 89–90
Gouldtowner, 45–46

Griffe, 6, 59
Guineas, 31, 43, 45, 48

Haití, 63, 66, 70, 118
Haliwa Saponi, 46
HAPA, 118
Hendrix, Jimi, 117
Hispanic, 5, 7–8, 12, 77, 115, 117, 124–26
Hispaniola, 118
Hitler, Adolph, 54

Ifekwunigwe, Jayne O., 78
Intercultural, 2, 24, 27, 31, 61, 71, 102, 128
Interfaith, 78
Interracial, 23, 27, 31, 44–47, 55, 61–62, 67, 69, 90, 101, 103, 111, 114, 116–17, 124, 126, 128, 131, 135
Islam, 39, 40, 44–45
Isle Brevelle, 47, 64–65, 67, 70
Italian, 12, 23, 43, 48, 73, 77–85, 88
Italy, 4, 20, 47, 74, 81, 83, 84, 88, 106

Jackson Whites, 38, 46, 52
Jamestown, 2, 4, 94–95, 97
Jim Crow, 13

Kelley, Matt, 125, 127

Laing, Sandra, 111, 113, 114
Latin American, 7
Latino, 5, 7–8, 12, 77, 88, 115–16
Legislation, 50, 55, 66, 78, 101, 123, 126
Lenni-Lennape, 91
Limpieza de sangre, 80
Locklear, Heather, 50, 53
Lost Colony of Roanoke. *See* Colony of Roanoke
Louisiana, 8, 13–14, 20, 44, 46–47, 59, 61–66, 68–74, 82–83, 130
Louisiana Purchase, 8, 62–62
Loving Day, 124, 129
Loving v. Virginia, 124
Lumbee, 21, 46, 49, 50–51, 53, 56

Manumission, 45
Mattaponi, 94–95, 97–98
MAVIN, 2, 124–27, 129
Medici, House of, 74, 81, 84–85

Meherin, 96–97
Melrose, 65, 66, 73
Melungeon, 4, 17, 34, 36, 37, 40, 44–46, 48, 51, 53, 56, 94, 111, 128–29
Mestizaje, 78, 87
Mestizo, 3–4, 7–8, 12, 30, 116
Metis, 4, 8, 130
Metoyer, 64–67, 70
México, 16, 63, 65, 70, 80
Miscegenation, 5, 7, 28, 66, 79–80, 123
Mitsawokett, 91
Mixed blood, 3–4, 35, 49, 91, 109, 112–13
Mixed race, 6–8, 12, 15, 21, 30–31, 33–34, 36, 41, 43, 46, 48, 51–52, 55–56, 60–62, 66, 69–71, 73–74, 77–78, 87, 89, 101, 103–9, 110, 113, 115–16, 118–19, 124–28, 130, 132, 136
Monacan, 56
Monacan Confederacy. *See* Monacan
Mongrelization, 55
Moor, 31, 33–34, 40, 43, 44–45, 89
Moorish, 33
Mulatto, 1, 6, 11–12, 30, 32, 35, 39, 48, 52, 59, 79, 91, 93–94, 102, 110, 116, 120, 129–30
Multiracial, 2, 4–8, 20–21, 27, 29–30, 41, 45–46, 48, 72, 77–81, 83, 85, 88, 90, 92, 102–3, 109, 111, 118–19, 125, 127–29, 132, 136
Mythology, 52

Nansemond, 94, 98
Natchez, 47, 70
Natchitoches, 47, 64–65, 70
Natirah, 129–30
Native American, 2–8, 12, 16–22, 30, 32, 37, 40–41, 44, 46, 48–52, 55–56, 59–60, 70, 80, 83, 89, 91–95, 98, 111, 115–16, 118
Negroes, 1, 2–3, 5, 35–36, 47, 56, 59, 62, 63, 65, 88, 98, 126
Nigger, 29, 33, 45, 52, 91, 114, 115, 116
North Carolina, 34–35, 40, 46, 48–50, 92, 94–95, 102, 115
Nottoway, 45, 96–97

Obama, Barack, 109–11
O'Brien, Soledad, 117, 123
Octoroon, 4, 6, 30, 32, 59, 79
One-drop rule, 11, 13–14, 119

Pamunkey, 56, 94, 96, 98, 115
Panamanian, 118
Passing, 11, 15, 19, 22, 54, 71
Pequot, 98–99
Phipps, Susie Guillory, 14
Placage, 67–68
Plantation, 3, 22, 31, 45–48, 65–66, 70, 73, 83, 117
Planters, 66, 70
Plecker, Walter Ashby, 54
Plessy v. Ferguson, 13
Pocahontas, 56, 94
Portugal, 4, 45–47, 80, 88, 106
Portuguese, 7–8, 17, 23, 31, 33–36, 41, 51, 60–62, 80, 81, 84, 116–17
Powhatan, 94–96
Powhatan confederacy, 94, 95
Powwow, 15, 16, 96
Puerto Rico, 70

Quadroon, 4, 6, 30, 32, 59, 67, 68, 79
Quilombos, 117

Racism, 20, 33, 36, 39, 48, 79, 81–82, 85, 101, 109, 112, 130
Ramapo Mountain People, 38–39, 43, 46, 52
Ramapough. *See* Ramapo Mountain People
Rappahannock, 56, 94, 95, 97, 98, 115
Reconciliation, 106, 109
Red Bone, 31, 33, 44, 46, 47
Reneges, 60
Rhiannon, 132
Robeson County, 35, 46, 49–50
Romany, 21, 36–37
Royalty: European, 78, 83; Italian, 78, 81, 83

Sanger, Margaret, 54, 56
Santo Domingo, 3
Sicily, 79, 81
Slave, 5, 32, 39–40, 45–46, 48, 50–52, 59–63, 65–68, 79, 92–93, 102, 113, 116–17

Slavery, 3, 40, 44, 46, 55, 59–63, 65, 93, 102
Smith, Captain John, 95
Sorry Day, 105
South Africa, 5, 22, 23, 106, 112–14
Spain, 4, 16, 20, 45, 68, 72, 80, 106, 116
Spanish, 7, 20, 23, 34, 45, 47–48, 59, 61–64, 67–68, 70, 73, 80–81, 115–17, 124
Stolen Generation, 5, 101–6
Sub-Saharan African, 4–5, 21–22, 48, 78, 83
Surnames, 20, 33, 38–39, 43, 45, 47–48, 51–53, 70, 89, 91, 116
SWIRL, 130, 131

Tan, 15, 22, 27–41, 44, 60, 90, 130
Tangosmaos, 60–61
Tennessee, 17, 20, 34–35, 46, 51
Third Reich, 54
Tignon Law, 69
Topaz Club, 132
Torres Strait Islander, 27, 103, 105
Trail of Tears, 16, 17, 92
Transracial adoption, 23, 125, 127–28, 135
Treaty, 82, 94–95, 97
Tribal, 3, 34, 38, 45, 49, 90, 92–93, 95–97
Tribe, 3, 16, 22, 34, 38, 46, 49, 50, 52, 56, 89–98, 116
Triracial, 2, 4, 5, 7–8, 12, 14, 21, 24, 27, 33–34, 36, 38, 40, 43–53, 83, 88, 97, 102, 109, 130, 136
Turkey, 4, 46, 51
Turkish, 23, 33–34
Turner, Tina, 117
Tuscarora, 50, 52, 53, 92, 96

Une placée, 67–68
United States Census Bureau, 77
Upper Mattaponi, 97

Venezuela, 117
Virginia, 2–4, 34–35, 40, 43, 45–46, 48, 50–51, 54–56, 80, 88, 92, 94–97, 102, 115, 123–24
Virginia Company, 4, 80, 94
Virginia's Racial Integrity Act, 55

Wahunsunacock, 95
We Sorts, 46, 52
West Africa, 20–22, 65, 70, 73, 79, 106, 116, 126
Whiteness, 36, 41, 44, 78
Woods, Tiger, 110, 118–19

Yucca Plantation, 65–66, 73

Zambo, 8, 115–18, 120
Zydeco, 47, 70–73

About the Author

STEPHANIE ROSE BIRD is an independent scholar and anthropologist. She is herself tri-racial, and has been interviewed on the topic by media including ABC, National Public Radio, and the Public Broadcast System.